The People Speak

Navajo Folk Art

THE PEOPLE SPEAK

NAVAJO FOLK ART

By Chuck and Jan Rosenak
Photographs by Lynn Lown

Northland Publishing

Cover and Frontispiece Art: Delbert Buck, *Navajo Couple on Horseback,* 1991. Mixed media (carved and painted wood, wire glasses, beadwork, turquoise jewelry, aluminum foil, leather, feathers, cloth, horse hair), man measures 26" x 20 ^{1}/2" x 7 ^{1}/2", woman measures 20" x 19" x 7".
Title Page Art: Ronald Malone (see page 95).
Table of Contents Art (clockwise from top left): Tom Yazzie (see page 10), Dennis Hathale (see page 87), Myra Tso Kaye (see page 115), and Robin Willeto (see page 60).
Back Cover Art: Lulu Yazzie (see page 103).

First Edition, 1994
ISBN 0-87358-565-8
Library of Congress Catalog Card Number 93-40024

Cataloging in Publication Data
Rosenak, Chuck.
The people speak : Navajo folk art / by Chuck and Jan Rosenak ; photographs by Lynn Lown. — 1st ed.
p.   cm.
Includes bibliographical references and index.
ISBN 0-87358-565-8 : $40.00
1. Navajo Indians—Art. 2. Folk art—Southwest, New. 3. Navajo Indians—Social life and customs.
I. Rosenak, Jan. I. Title.
E99.N3R65 1994
704'.03972—dc20   93-40024

Manufactured in Hong Kong by Sing Cheong
Art Photographer: Lynn Lown (unless otherwise noted)
Artist Photographer: Chuck Rosenak (unless otherwise noted)
Designer: Julie Sullivan, Sullivan Scully Design Group
Art Directors: David Jenney and Trina Stahl
Production Coordinator: Lisa Brownfield
Editors: Betti Albrecht, Erin Murphy, and Diana Clark Lubick

4-93/5M/0437

To Dr. Robert Bishop (1938–1991), Director, Museum of American Folk Art,
New York City, from 1977 to 1991. Bob was our friend and our mentor,
as well as an early supporter of contemporary Navajo folk art.

To Elizabeth Albrecht (1957–1993), Editor-in-Chief of Northland Publishing.
When Betti wrote us that *of course* she was interested in Navajo folk art,
we knew we had a worthwhile project.
Her sensitivity and insight were of great assistance.

Contents

1 Introduction

20 The Eastern Region

64 The Central Region

108 The Western Region

Foreword

The People Speak: Navajo Folk Art features work by forty-two self-taught Native American folk artists. These artists were selected from hundreds of contemporaries over approximately sixteen million acres (twenty-five thousand square miles) in New Mexico, Arizona, and Utah. Today, the Navajo Nation represents not only the largest Native American tribe in the United States, but also one whose artistic and cultural achievements deserve greater attention. This publication is a visual testimony to the tremendous vitality and originality of this indigenous folk art tradition.

For many years, the traditional perception of Navajo art by the American and European public has been largely in terms of exquisite Navajo textiles and silver work. This new book challenges our established perceptions by visually presenting the diversity of the innovative genres (wood carvings, clay figures, fired pottery, pictorial weavings, and cardboard) being pursued by these artists. In addition, the extensive use of photographic documentation demonstrates the inextricable link of this art form to the socio-cultural fabric of everyday Navajo life. Clearly, this book will impact a greater public understanding of Navajo culture as a force in contemporary American society. The achievements and relevance of these Navajo artists deserve our recognition as an exciting native artistic and cultural expression.

Through their years of field work, the authors are greatly furthering the pioneering efforts of earlier exhibitions at the St. Louis Craft Alliance (1987), the Wheelwright Museum (1988), and the Museum of Northern Arizona (1990). The authors' recent publication of the *Museum of American Folk Art Encyclopedia of Twentieth-Century American Folk Art and Artists* (1990) has generated tremendous popular interest in contemporary folk art and the rich diversity of regional expressions.

Chuck and Jan Rosenak's current search for an indigenous American art form is an important part of an ongoing dialogue in American art and literature. The contemporary Navajo artists featured in this volume share a strong impulse to artistically record aspects of their surroundings and experiences. Their works are visual representations of inner feelings attempting, as stated by the nineteenth century poet William Cullen Bryant, "a sincere communication of their moral and intellectual being." This individual expression is perhaps the most poignant characteristic and reminder of the pluralism of our society.

Inevitably, this search for indigenous art forms raises the question, What are the precise qualities that characterize American art? Although there is no all-encompassing answer to this recurring question, the writer Lloyd Goodrich states in his searching essay, *What Is American in American Art,* "There are many diverse qualities that can be called characteristically American, for ours is pluralist art, the expression of a democratic society, giving free rein to wide individualism in artistic creating."[1] Indeed, this quality is a hallmark not only of our society but also of the achievements of the Navajo artist.

The changes in style, function, and taste throughout American history reflect the subjective interests of successive societies. Artists similarly have arrived at new visual statements by responding to the realities of our physical environment and realizing that there is beauty in the American commonplace. This artistic tradition is organic, and has a firm place in our national consciousness. As one critic stated, "A Navajo experiences beauty most poignantly in creating it and expressing it, not in observing it or preserving it. The experience of beauty is dynamic; it flows to one and from one; it is found not in things, but in relationships among things."[2]

The Navajo folk artists in this volume have created striking definitions of their environment and experience and the relationship of these to their own characters. Our native environment enabled these individuals to arrive at certain truths. Ultimately, their works exemplify the persistence of native themes and values, and they are a rich memoir of individual expressions in the ongoing quest for a valid American aesthetic. In addition, these Navajo artists can teach us a great deal about their unique culture and society, allowing us to enjoy their rich creative legacy and artistic beauty.

JOSEPH S. CZESTOCHOWSKI
Director, Cedar Rapids Museum of Art

1 Lloyd Goodrich, *What Is American in American Art* (New York: M. Knoedler and Co., 1979).
2 Gary Witherspoon, *Language and Art in the Navajo Universe* (Ann Arbor: University of Michigan Press, 1977), p. 178.

Mamie Deschillie, *Buffalo*, 1987. Mixed media (cardboard, paint, wool, sequins, glass beads, doll eyes), 35" x 38".

Preface

The scope of this book on Navajo folk art is wide-ranging. It includes self-taught artists who create paintings, drawings, sculptures, assemblages, pottery, and pictorial rugs. We believe that the Navajo folk artists included in this volume are among the most innovative folk artists of the twentieth century.

Because of the vastness of the Navajo Nation, we have divided it, solely for convenience, into three regions: eastern, central, and western. Maps illustrate the reservation as a whole, as well as each individual region. General information concerning the area is provided in the introduction to the regions. Where appropriate, these introductions also contain information about particular types of folk art of that region (pottery and pictorial rugs, for example) and traders who have been influential in encouraging the artists. The artists have been placed in the region in which they live or work.

There is at least one example in color to illustrate the work of each artist included here. In many instances, the work is represented by two or more color plates. A descriptive caption accompanies each plate. Black-and-white pictures of the artists are also shown.

We have included considerable biographical data in the account of each individual artist. Additional statistical information (date of birth, residence) is set forth in Appendix A. We have also provided an account of the Navajo origin legend (Appendix B), a glossary of terms, and an extensive bibliography subdivided by category.

We hope you enjoy reading and using *The People Speak: Navajo Folk Art* as much as we have enjoyed putting it together.

Introduction

The Search for an American Style of Art

Our journey into contemporary folk art began on New York's Madison Avenue in 1973. That year, the Whitney Museum of American Art included in its prestigious Biennial of Contemporary Art a small carving of Adam and Eve by the Kentucky preacher Edgar Tolson, who blew his church off its foundation because his parishioners "can't live it" (the word of the Lord). This was the first piece of contemporary folk art we had seen and the only one, to our knowledge, ever included in a Whitney Biennial. We were captivated. But we were told that if we went to Campton to visit the artist, we might be shot. We were also told that bootleg bourbon was distilled in Campton and that the "natives" were unfriendly to strangers.

We went to Campton. We smelled the mash brewing, we drank the bourbon, and Edgar Tolson welcomed us into his trailer home on top of a mountain. We met our first folk artist on that hill in Kentucky twenty years ago.

We didn't realize it at first, but what we had begun was a search for an American art form. The art being shown on Madison Avenue and Michigan Avenue was deriva-

Opposite: Fannie Pete, *Statue of Liberty*, c. 1992. Pictorial rug, commercial yarn, 35 ¹/₂" x 21 ¹/₂".

tive of European/American academic styles. It was hyped by the museum-gallery-collector (socially smart and acceptable) art scene and forgotten when the next style or fad came along. To tag along with the art scene was fun. It gave us a sense of belonging to be in on the latest gossip, to buy a work in the current style, and to be an insider in the art world. But when we met Edgar Tolson, we knew we were in the presence of what could only be a truly original American artist.

Most of the American folk art of the last century came out of immigrant-generated craft traditions. The individual artist's identity was often lost; one Amish quilt maker's work is similar to another; one sweet grass basket may just about equal another; one itinerant portrait painter may be almost as good as any other. In these circumstances,

1

Edgar Tolson, *Expulsion*, c. 1973.
Carved and painted white poplar and
pencil, 14" x 19 ¹/₂" x 6 ¹/₂".

the artist becomes anonymous—signing pieces only rarely.

What collectors seemed to look for in folk art was the craft or the utilitarian value of an object and not the art. From the very beginning, we were looking for art—something wonderful, even idiosyncratic, that makes one object stand out in a crowd of objects. Good old reliable Webster affixes the phrase "creative imagination" to the definition of the word "art." Where there's art, there are artists. "Anonymous" was not good enough for us—anonymous could be anybody. Folk artists do not have press agents, and they do not hand out neatly printed fact sheets. They are self-taught in art, though they may have learned their craft (carpentry and weaving, for instance) from family or society. Because they are isolated from, and generally unaware of, the "art scene," they may not even know that they are making art.

Art mirrors society and the times an artist lives in. Contemporary art, therefore, mirrors contemporary America and tells us something about our lives and our country. We believe there is a universality to be found in the personal visions of folk artists that adds a dimension often left out of standard accounts of contemporary art.

What prompted our journey? We felt that if we could find the folk art of America, we would discover what this country was all about and learn something about ourselves in the process. That's why we set out on our voyage of discovery. Our adventure led us from the mountains of Kentucky, to the hollers of West Virginia, to Chicago's Cabrini Green, to the delta of the Mississippi River, and west to the shores of the Pacific. Wherever we traveled, we discovered two universal truths: (1) that the compulsion to communicate through the medium of art exists in the human soul even though the creator may not recognize his or her work as art; and (2) that virtually all artists welcome the outsider and the opportunity to share their visions.

At first (in the 1940s), contemporary American folk art was thought to exist only in the East.[1] By the early 1970s, a few pockets of isolated folk art were acknowledged west of the Mississippi River.[2] By 1980, most contemporary folk art was thought to be southern in origin. We were the first to write about contemporary folk art as a universal American art style—on the cutting edge of contemporary art.[3] And our own horizons were constantly expanding.

On a house-hunting trip to Santa Fe in December 1983, we discovered a small exhibition of mud toys by Mamie Deschillie and Elsie Benally and the carvings of Johnson Antonio at the Wheelwright Museum of the American Indian. We knew then that our next journey had to be to the Navajo Nation—one of the last outposts of America's shrinking West.

The boundaries of the present Navajo Nation were established by the Treaty of 1868 (and subsequently enlarged by various executive orders and acts of Congress). The area ceded to the Navajo was useless, as far as the white man was concerned—it had few minerals, insufficient grass to support cattle, and precious little water. Today, the reservation has about sixteen million acres, a vast portion of which is presently in Arizona and New Mexico, extending northward into Utah.

Interest in contemporary folk art—including Navajo—has increased dramatically in the last two decades. When we started our journey on the mountaintop in Kentucky, there probably weren't more then six people in America interested in taking a similar route. There were only two commercial galleries in the field. By 1993, there were as many as ten thousand collectors of twentieth-century folk art,[4] and there was an army of pickers supporting more than a hundred galleries. We coined the term "contemporary Navajo folk art" in December of 1983 when we saw the show at the Wheelwright Museum of the American Indian. We were almost by ourselves visiting Navajo artists in the *Dinétah* (Navajo Nation) in 1984. Today, the word is out. Indian Trader Jack Beasley (to mention just one) has a list of over fifteen hundred collectors of Navajo folk art (lawyers, doctors, authors, museum curators, and anthropologists), and his list includes dealers in many major cities who have additional lists. We couldn't keep contemporary Navajo folk art a secret if we tried—but we have always shared our discoveries.

In the summer of 1986, our good friends Barbara and Ed Okun asked us to curate a contemporary folk art show at the Craft Alliance Gallery and Education Center in St. Louis. To this day, I do not know why I replied: "Yes, if you let us show Navajo folk art."

With the expert help of Barbara Jedda, the gallery director, we put together a small exhibition (Folk Art of the People: Navajo Works, which ran from September 4 through September 26, 1987) and a thin catalogue, now a collector's item. Some of the artists in this book—Johnson Antonio, Mamie Deschillie, Dan Hot, the Hathale family, Faye Tso, and the Willeto family—were included in the earlier show. The St. Louis exhibition was the first general survey of contemporary Navajo folk art, and it was a critical success in the local media. We were off and running.

In 1988, we were instrumental in persuading the Wheelwright Museum of the American Indian in Santa Fe to present a somewhat larger showing of contemporary Navajo innovative art. The resulting exhibition, curated by Bruce Bernstein and Susan Brown McGreevy, ended up with the title Anii Ánáádaalyaa' Ígíí (Recent Ones That Are Made). While the title was difficult to pronounce and even harder to spell, the objects were well received.

Again, in 1990, we participated in a still larger showing of Navajo work at the Museum of Northern Arizona in Flagstaff, curated by Dr. Trudy Thomas. By this time, we knew that Navajo folk art was on its way.

In the same year, our Museum of American Folk Art Encyclopedia of Twentieth-Century American Art and Artists was published. It included the most celebrated artists in the field—among them were eight of the Navajo artists in this book.

It is time for a book on contemporary Navajo folk art. It is time to give these American artists a measure of the recognition they deserve.

The Navajo artists included in this book and in the exhibition were chosen by the same criteria that we used to identify Adam and Eve's Expulsion by Edgar Tolson as a great piece of American sculpture. We have defined folk art as work by untrained, self-taught artists that is nonutilitarian, highly personal, even idiosyncratic. The craft may be derived from communal traditions, but something personal must be added to qualify it as art. In other words, the craft may be learned, but the art is self-taught.

While decisions based on aesthetic considerations are, of necessity, subjective, we have followed essentially the same guidelines for twenty years, and these were the guidelines used for inclusion of artists in this book:

1. Since biographical information is a key element in determining the authenticity and self-taught nature of the work, anonymous works have been excluded.

2. The artist must have a recognizable body of work and have been included in books, articles, museum exhibitions, or gallery showings. In other words, the artists have all been exposed to some other critical acclaim in addition to our personal subjective judgment.

3. The artists must produce objects that demonstrate a personal creative vision.
Their work has to stand out in a crowd of objects. We did not look for utilitarian objects that are part of the Navajo material culture.

4. We have not included ceremonial objects for two reasons: (1) their production is so prescribed by tradition that they are not art in the sense of No. 3 above; and (2) out of sensitivity to the Navajo.

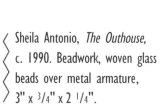

Sheila Antonio, *The Outhouse*, c. 1990. Beadwork, woven glass beads over metal armature, 3" x 3/4" x 2 1/4".

We have encountered far more artists than we were able to include in this book. Many other potters, for example, come to mind—Lucy Leuppe McKelvey, Jimmy and Clara Wilson, George Slick, Lorena Bartlett, Mary Lou Davis, Penny Emerson, and Cecilia and John Whiterock, to name a few.[5] Another artist who deserves special mention is Rose Williams (born 1915). She is a living treasure of the Shonto/Cow Springs area who has taught successive generations the Navajo tradition of pottery making—among them Faye Tso, Silas Claw, Louise Goodman, and Lorena Bartlett. Her children, Alice Cling, Sue Ann Williams, and Susie Williams Crank, and her daughter-in-law Lorraine Williams are all recognized potters.

Necessity has forced us to limit our discussion of potters to those we feel have created a significant body of folk art, those most deserving of inclusion in a first general survey of Navajo folk art. However, we have personally collected the work of all of the potters mentioned above and recommend them to anyone interested in Navajo pottery.

The number of outstanding weavers is even more staggering. The Navajo are well known for their intricately designed rugs. Our best guess is that there are several thousand Navajo women who regularly work at a loom. But pictorial rugs (weavings intended to hang on a wall) are not as well known and are a fine example of Navajo folk art. Therefore, we have limited our inclusion of weavers to individuals like Florence Riggs and Linda Nez, who typify the stretch from tradition to contemporary, from fine craft to folk art.

Most of the pictorials produced today can be broken down into now-traditional categories, such as sandpaintings, Trees of Life, and the ever-popular trucks, Yeis, birds, and flags. But these pieces do not meet our criteria because they are all copies or repeated patterns. We were looking for original art. We believe that there are less than ten pictorial Navajo artists weaving truly original designs, and we have attempted to find and visit them all.

It is often stated that there is no well-defined tradition of woodcarving among the Navajo like there is among their Hopi neighbors. Because traders to the Navajo were not prepared to acquire this form of art, we feel that carving was not encouraged as other art forms were. Tradition and taboo have played a role as well.

Johnson Antonio, who began carving out of an impulse he cannot explain, has broken through the myth that Navajos can't carve. He is the founding father of a new Navajo tradition of figurative carving—one that should be watched closely in the future. And many of the other carvers in the book, like Ray Growler and Tom Yazzie, have also been responsible for breaking new ground. Tom Yazzie, one of the first to carve a set of Yeibichai dancers, believes that he did not lose his eyesight, as predicted by the medicine men, because of his "respect for the subject matter." And because of his sense of respect, he will only carve Yeis after the first frost and before the spring thaw when the masked dancers appear.

There are other artists in this book who have revived traditions and added new life to them (Mamie Deschillie's and Elsie Benally's mud toys, for example) and others who appear to have founded new artistic traditions, as yet not fully developed or understood.

The journey into the world of Navajo folk art has been our pleasure. We have explored the three regions of the Dinétah—east, central and west—from Nageezi to unspoiled Sweetwater, the folk art capital of Arizona. Wherever we have gone, we have found Americans free to express themselves in whatever medium was at hand. What we have found is truly remarkable and definitely part of the great American art of our century.

We were the outsiders, privileged to be welcomed into the homes and lives of artists wherever we went. *The People Speak: Navajo Folk Art* is a continuation of our adventure in dirt-track America—seeking the best in contemporary folk art. We hope that this book will serve as a milestone of discovery for our readers and that further work in the field will follow.

The Diné [6]

On a turbulent night in October of 1992, artist Tom Yazzie escorted us to observe the final, all-night masked dances of a Yeibichai ceremony conducted by his famous medicine man brother, Alfred W. Yazzie. Hard, cold rain blew into the windshield, obscuring the countryside. The dirt road winding three miles uphill to the camp where the ceremony was in progress, near Fort Defiance, was door-handle deep in mud; it oozed in onto the floor mat of the car.

When we approached the hogan, where prayers were being chanted, mud sucked our boots deep into cold slime. The shadows of perhaps two hundred Navajo men and women (many had been at this place for nine days) were elongated by ten or twelve bonfires of sparking cedar logs that fought the darkness. Frankly, I was nervous. But the ceremony was nothing like anything that we had seen before, and the audience was quiet, respectful, sober, and welcoming.

Opposite: Charlie Willeto, *Male and Female Navajo Figures,* c. 1962-64. Carved and painted wood, male measures 66 1/4" x 16 1/2" x 10 1/4", female measures 66 1/2" x 16 1/4" x 14 1/4". Photograph courtesy of the Smithsonian Institution.

The dancing began around eleven o'clock at night when the sky miraculously cleared and stars showed through the clouds. The dance was like something out of former centuries. Firelight reflected in mirrors attached to the skirts of the Yei dancers, both men and women. They wore the traditional dark blue masks topped by eagle feathers three feet long. Their chants were powerful and rhythmic (a sort of falsetto, animal-yapping sound with intermittent shouts and shaking of gourd rattles). Unlike Pueblo dancers, they were not accompanied by drums in this ceremony. Tom Yazzie said that their songs were in an ancient language that even he could not exactly translate. The sound is intentionally unlike that of other Navajo singing, since it is the voices of the gods that are heard in Yeibichai chants.[7]

There were several sets of dancers. Each new set to appear stood in a line and saluted the patient and the medicine man (who came out of the hogan for this purpose) with a kind of medieval salutation-bow. They, in turn, blessed the dancers with cornmeal. The dancers performed, sometimes in a line, as usually depicted in Navajo art, but sometimes wheeling in intricate patterns. The dancing and prayers continued to first light. As dawn approached, Talking God appeared to lead the dancers, wearing his majestic white mask decorated with a single corn plant.

The patient had an earache or growth in his ear. We later learned that he was cured and returned to his job in Albuquerque. We knew that we were privileged outsiders and were grateful for the opportunity to witness some of the mystery that makes the Diné unique and that is a part of their art.

Tom Yazzie, *Yeibichai Dancers* (detail), c. 1991-92. Carved and painted cottonwood, figures range in height from 2 1/2" to 10".

Navajo History

The town of Fort Defiance is east of Ganado. It was built in the heart of Navajo country in 1851 as an attempt to stop Indian raiding. In 1863, after various earlier skirmishes, a "scorched earth campaign" against the Navajo was initiated under the leadership of Colonel Christopher "Kit" Carson. Crops were destroyed and livestock was slaughtered. In January of 1864, Carson attacked their last stronghold, Canyon de Chelly. All options exhausted, most Navajos surrendered; others hid in remote places.

In March of 1864, the Navajos who had surrendered began the infamous march of more than 300 miles to Fort Sumner, New Mexico, and the Bosque Redondo. This trek is known to Navajos as the "Long Walk." Along the way, hundreds were left behind, dead or dying on the trail.

The government envisioned that Bosque Redondo would become self-supporting through agriculture. However, the land was bad, the crop yield poor, and the population grew rapidly (to about 8,500), thus taxing the Army's food supply.

Eventually, on June 1, 1868, a treaty was signed at Fort Sumner, the Treaty of 1868, establishing the Navajo Nation (subsequently enlarged by executive orders and acts of Congress). It was only a fraction of the size of the original homeland.

The Navajos remaining at Fort Sumner began their "Long Walk" home in June of 1868—to join their brethren who had taken refuge from the Army in remote places like Navajo Mountain.

When the Navajos returned from Bosque Redondo, the old wood and adobe fort in the town of Fort Defiance was mostly in ruins. Nevertheless, the federal government established the Navajo Agency and installed the first Indian Agent at Fort Defiance in an attempt to centralize control over this land.

The survivors of Bosque Redondo, without crops, livestock, homes, or weapons, together with those who had hidden, became the nucleus of the present Nation. Today, the Navajo is the largest Indian tribe in the United States, with more than 219,000 enrolled members (1990 census). The Navajo Nation encompasses approximately twenty-five thousand square miles (about sixteen million acres) in the states of Arizona, New Mexico, and Utah.

Central to the Navajo religion and culture are the four natural boundary markers of the Dinétah, the sacred mountains—Mount Hesperus (*Dibé Nitsaa*) on the north, Sierra Blanca Peak (*Sisnaajiní*) to the east, Mount Taylor (*Tsoodził*) on the south, and the San Francisco Peaks (*Dook'o'oosłiid*) near Flagstaff, Arizona, to the west. Each direction has its own spiritual meaning; these boundaries are part of the Navajo origin myth—the names of the mountains were given to the People by First Man. While none of these mountains is located on the present homeland, all of them dominate the landscape and can be viewed from various vantage points within the present-day Navajo Nation. The symbols of these sacred mountains, and the directions of the compass they represent, appear in sandpaintings and Navajo art.

The Traders

Congress, under President George Washington, passed a bill "for the protection of Indians" in 1796. This bill authorized the President "to establish trading houses" among the Indians. The earliest traders obtained the use of land without the requirement of paying rent and were licensed by the government. Today, traders are controlled through a series of regula-

Bill Nez, cartoon for trading post rug
(for Florence Riggs weaving),
c. 1992. Magic marker on cardboard,
20 1/2" x 24 1/2".

tions and by the terms of their leases. Because a reservation trader cannot accumulate equity in the land under his post, he is usually hesitant to spend large sums of money on capital improvements. Many traders made vast fortunes, but their wealth was not reinvested in upgrading their posts.

The first Indian trader to be licensed on the newly created Dinétah was Lehman Spiegelberg of Santa Fe, appointed by Major Theodore Dodd, the new Indian Agent at Fort Defiance, on August 28, 1868.

While many of the Indian Agents were ineffectual, Thomas Keam, an able administrator who became an important trader at Keams Canyon, took over the agency in 1870 during a serious drought. Keam pleaded with Washington for more sheep and supplies and successfully organized a Navajo police force to stop raiding.

In 1869, the year before Keam became agent, the Presbyterian Mission Board sent the first white teacher, Charity Gaston, to the Navajos at Fort Defiance. Construction of a boarding school there was authorized by Congress in 1879. By 1881, the railroad reached western New Mexico, resulting in an increasing number of trading posts. Today, Fort Defiance is a bustling small town. However, its importance has lessened somewhat since a neighboring town, Window Rock, became the capital of the Navajo Nation.

During the 1870s, commerce with the outside world was slowly established. First to develop was the blanket trade, which grew into a rug trade, and the demand grew steadily. In recent times, with the coming of paved roads and the universally present pickup truck, commerce is accelerating at a rapid rate. But historically, virtually all the weaver's trade and contact with the outside world was through the intermediary at the closest trading post. Even today, when one of the weavers of the western region was having trouble getting what she considered to be a fair price from the local trader, we suggested that she try a gallery in Santa Fe—and her answer was, "Where's Santa Fe?"

Because of this historically close relationship with the Indians, the trader could, in turn, sometimes dictate, based on his view of the market, the design and materials used in craft items—a concept we call "easy marketability." When a pattern proved popular with buyers, weavers were encouraged to repeat the general design. Today, the Crystal Trading

Post at the edge of the Chuska Mountains above Window Rock is in ruin, but in its heyday (1896–1911), J. B. Moore, the proprietor, circulated a catalogue to the eastern market, selling rugs and blankets by the pound, according to designs he favored. Crystal rugs are technically excellent (we've purchased a few), rugged, worth many times their original value today, but the artistry of their creators is largely missing. The idiosyncratic or innovative rug that did not please the trader often simply disappeared.

Illustrative of the daily activity still taking place on and near the Navajo Nation is the chain of Indian traders, dealers, and collectors. This chain—from trader to dealer to collector, finally to a museum—led to the preservation of the work of Charlie Willeto (page 54) and eventually to the realization of its importance by the art world.

The trader is the first point of contact between the Navajo artist and the rest of the world. If a market can't be found, the artist is discouraged and the work may be destroyed. Or even worse, the trader can say to the artist: "make it my way—I can sell this or that— but not what you have brought me." Easy marketability is a time-honored custom, but in some instances, it may destroy the innovative quality of the work (one of the essentials that elevates an object into the category of art). The link between artist and trader is thus important and, at the same time, fragile.

On the other hand, a trader can assist the artists in the pursuit of artists' visions. One present-day example is Bill Beaver (born 1925), the owner of Sacred Mountain Trading Post. While still in high school, Beaver decided he wanted to live free. He spent his summers among the Navajo, herding sheep for no pay. The GI Bill financed Beaver's degree in anthropology at the University of New Mexico.

"But I didn't know what an anthropologist is supposed to do," he said. "So, in about 1950, I got a job working for Reuben Heflin at the Shonto Trading Post [in Arizona]. Heflin traded in rugs and jewelry and wouldn't give pottery the time of day. However, I liked it. The work was crude, but each pot was a one-of-a-kind deal, and the ladies were no longer making plain utilitarian items. I thought that they were beginning to make art. Stanley A. Stubbs at the Museum of Northern Arizona agreed with me, and I brought Navajo pottery for what was then called their Western Arts and Crafts Annual, and it began to sell."[8]

By 1960, Beaver had married Dollie Long, a Navajo who makes bead jewelry, and had purchased the Sacred Mountain Trading Post from William Blevins for $45,000. "The ladies [and later men who broke the taboo against men potting, such as William Manygoats, Silas Claw, and others] from Shonto/Cow Springs followed me here," he explained. "At first, the potters had no idea of the dollar value because previously

Holy Girl, Standing Above the East and West Moon, Dennis Hathale, c. 1986. Mineral pigment on percale bedsheet (muslin), 43" x 35".

utilitarian Navajo pottery was seldom sold—just bartered among the Indians. We made the market and the more innovative the work, the better it sold. Potters like Alice Cling, Silas Claw, Betty Manygoats, and Louise Goodman became superstars."

In 1981, Beaver's well-documented collection of more than 250 pieces of Navajo pottery was acquired by the Arizona State Museum in Tucson; this is the most important collection available to the public. A number of pots from the Beaver collection were displayed by the museum in *Shonto Junction: Where Navajo Potteries Meet,* an exhibition that opened in 1990, continuing into 1993.

Clan Relationships

The Navajo Way is one of close-knit extended families sharing in the joys, blessings, and hard times of reservation life. Clan relationships are very important. The Navajo kinship system is based on matrilineal descent. Each Navajo belongs to the clan of his or her mother and is "born for" the father's clan. (There are sixty or more clans.) Navajos cannot marry a member of the same clan, even if there is no blood relationship. Clan members are often addressed as "brother," "sister," "aunt," "grandmother," etc., whether or not there is a biological relationship.

Some clans have become known for particular skills. The *Lók'aa'dine'é* (Reed People) clan in the Shonto/Cow Springs area has long been recognized for its pottery making, and many of the present-day potters or their spouses (such as Silas Claw, Faye Tso, Rose Williams, and Alice Cling) are members of this clan. Until recently, many of the artists did not sign their work. One person might make the ware, another decorate it, and a third family or clan member take it to a trader for sale. In these circumstances, the trader might attribute the work to the person who brought in the piece. This would not be a matter of concern to the family, but a collector could have difficulty in identifying the artists who actually made the piece. That situation is changing today, as more and more of the artists—potters, carvers, and weavers—are signing their art.

Religion

Even though many contemporary Navajos no longer live in hogans, these structures, with their doors facing the sunrise, are a part of ceremonial and cultural life. When used as a residence, the family often sleeps in one room on cots or beds arranged against the walls around a central smoke hole. If a person dies in the hogan, the *chindi* or spirit is thought to be present, a hole is made in the north wall (the direction of evil) to allow for removal of the body, and the structure may be abandoned.

Among the Navajo, "religion" is not something separate, but a part of their daily life. The universe is regarded as an orderly, all-inclusive, unitary system of interrelated elements, each of which has its place and function. *Hózhǫ*, often translated as "beauty," "peace," or "harmony," is the desired state, the central idea in Navajo thinking and values.

The Native American Church, sometimes called the Peyote Cult by outsiders, emphasizes the unity of Indians and their distinctness from others. This ideology spread to the Navajo around the middle of this century. The church's Navajo membership has grown steadily since that time. While there are several organizations, most of the members belong the Native American Church of Navajoland. In general, peyote use is prohibited by the Navajo Tribal Council, but an exception is provided for Native American Church ceremonial use.

At first, there was fear that the traditional ceremonial system might decline as a result of the spread of the Native American Church. This has not happened. Church members have remained active in traditional ceremonies. Some medicine men, in fact, perform both types of ceremonies. (See, for example, Roger Hathale, page 82.)

Taboos

There is a general feeling among the Navajo that it can bring bad luck to carve a human or religious figure. If the carving was inaccurate or destroyed or broken, bad luck could follow for both the creator and the person or spirit depicted. Because of a fear that a carved image resembling some family member might be broken (perhaps causing the death of that individual), carved images are rarely made by the Navajo.

Another concern is the ignoring of the ritual restriction against recreating Yei figures, which might cause blindness or other harm. There are many other taboos and omens. Owls, which appear in the carvings of Charlie Willeto and Edith Herbert John, "are both good and bad," according to medicine man Alfred Yazzie. "They have great wisdom and knowledge, but you do not want them to visit your home or ceremony. If an owl hoots above your home or hogan, it means the family who lives there will soon hear bad news." Only a few taboos are actually rooted in religion, the greatest number having been handed down on the basis of some past unfavorable event.

It is not surprising that myths, legends, and taboos developed in this isolated land of mysterious beauty. Spirits dance at first light on craggy peaks, on the lonesome howl of the coyote at full moon, and are brought to Earth on the wings of the magnificent bald eagle, whose feathers are sacred to the Diné. And is there truth in the legends? Do witches practice their magic in this strange and beautiful place? One of the most persistent tales is that of the skinwalker—an evil witch who is part-man, part-wolf.

Author Tony Hillerman doesn't believe in them. He tells the story of a man who shot at a skinwalker robbing his chicken coop, and a neighbor turned up the next morning with a bullet wound. But almost every Navajo we met has seen or heard of skinwalkers. Candeleria Brown, who works behind the desk at the Holiday Inn at Chinle, for instance, has seen them.

Indian trader Jack Beasley has seen one. "It ran 'longside my pickup one midnight on the long hill climbing south of Farmington," he said. "It was half-wolf with red beady eyes trying to hypnotize me. The skinwalker said, 'I'll get you Jack!' I drove right through it."

Anonymous,
Navajo Yei Mask,
c. 1930. Mixed media
(deerskin, horsehair, ground
turquoise pigment, wool, gourd,
and abalone shell), 17" x 11".

Jan and I have never seen a skinwalker. But, remember, as you read this book and look at the illustrations, that these apparitions are just as much a part of the lives and art of the Navajo as the legends of Appalachia, the Georgia hills, or the Mississippi Delta are to many of the people of those regions. Why is it that the *Bilagáana* (white man) will not occupy the thirteenth story of a building, or walk under a ladder? Why do we pick four-leaf clovers, throw salt over a shoulder, knock on wood? When there is lightning and heavy thunder, a mother in the South will tell her small children that "it's the devil beating his wife." A female devil appears in the carvings of Southern artists like Ronald Cooper (from Kentucky) and Sulton Rogers (from Mississippi). Charley Kinney painted the "haints" of Kentucky. We found southern visionaries painting Bible stories from a book they couldn't read. J. B. Murry and Z. B. Armstrong are prime examples of this genre called "visionary art." When we talk about the visions of a Navajo artist, you have to realize that most of them are not Christians; their visions are Navajo in origin and do not include Christ, angels, or the devil.

Taboos can have an impact on the art. Artist Tom Yazzie has attempted to avoid the taboos against carving by making certain that his figures are as accurate as possible, down to the last tiny detail. Over the years, the list of restrictions associated with pottery making have become lengthy and more difficult to observe. Pottery must be made away from other people. A potter should not swear, have bad thoughts, or jump across ditches. Menstruating women may not make pottery. Pottery should not be exposed to drafts.

In fact, so many restrictions and taboos grew up surrounding Navajo pottery that some women were afraid to try their hand at it for fear that they would unknowingly break a taboo, an action with potentially serious consequences. At the very least, the pot could crack or break. At the other end of the spectrum, an illness, perhaps blindness, could result.

The decoration of pottery with appliquéd or painted figures was discouraged in the western region. This restriction is similar to the one that prohibits the carving of a recognizable figure from wood—the fear that harm will come to the person (or spirit) depicted if the wood should be broken or the carving prove to be imperfect.

Anonymous, *Navajo Female Yei Mask*, c. 1910. Mixed media (ground turquoise on deerskin, horsehair, bead band, Hubbell glass trade bead earrings), 12" x 10".

Artist Ida Sahmie put it another way, "If I paint a Yei figure on a pot, and then burn him in fire [firing the ware], that would be bad, but I have had a 'sing' to protect me." The same type of prohibition is thought by some traditional Navajo to apply to picture-taking; they may not allow their picture to be taken for fear that part of their spirit will be lost. All of these traditions are interrelated, and all of these restrictions, beliefs, and taboos differ slightly from area to area and person to person. In total, however, they create a community barrier against innovation.

At times, a traditional taboo can introduce an artistic element. Navajo pottery, for example, has a beaded design element, called a *biyo'*, on the rim. A small break in the *biyo'* (similar to the break in Navajo baskets) is called *atiin*, "the way out." Mae Adson, a relative of potter Rose Williams, explained the taboo against decoration and the reason for the break as follows: "The Anasazi started to over decorate their pottery, and the wind destroyed them, because of that. That's why we are told not to decorate pottery. The coils shouldn't come together. That opening is for life. If you make it come together it might shorten your life."[9]

The horny (horned) toad or lizard is also protected by a taboo. Harming a horny toad (or even representing one) may bring trouble, according to Navajo tradition. Yet artists challenge these taboos daily—some confidently, some with caution.

The Navajo Way

The present Navajo Nation has changed substantially in recent years. There have been changes in the economy, government, health care, and especially in education. While adapting in many ways to current conditions in the country, the Navajo continue to live according to the "Navajo Way." A prayer that gives the Navajo strength and inspiration is uttered at the close of traditional ceremonies and business affairs. It is as follows:

In beauty may we dwell.
In beauty may we walk.
In beauty may our male kindred dwell.
In beauty may our female kindred dwell.
In beauty may it rain on our young men.
In beauty may it rain on our chiefs.
In beauty may it rain on us.

In beauty may our corn grow.
In the trail of pollen may it rain.
In beauty may we walk.
The beauty is restored.
The beauty is restored.
The beauty is restored.
The beauty is restored.

Notes to Introduction

1 See Sidney Janis, *They Taught Themselves: American Primitive Painters of the 20th Century* (New York: Dial Press, 1942). Most of the artists included in Janis's book were from New York and the Northeast; all but one lived in the East.

2 Herbert W. Hemphill, Jr. and Julia Weissman, *Twentieth Century American Folk Art and Artists* (New York: E. P. Dutton, 1974).

3 Chuck and Jan Rosenak, *Museum of American Folk Art Encyclopedia of Twentieth-Century American Folk Art and Artists* (New York: Abbeville Press, 1990).

4 Estimate provided by Dr. Warren Lowe, a collector and author. His wife, Sylvia, an attorney, has decorated her office with Mamie Deschillie cutouts. (See Bibliography, *Baking in the Sun: Visionary Images from the South* and *It'll Come True: Eleven Artists First and Last).*

5 For a more general study of contemporary Navajo pottery, see Russell P. Hartman and Jan Musial, *Navajo Pottery: Traditions and Innovations* (Flagstaff: Northland Publishing, 1987).

6 Navajo or "The People." Also spelled "Dineh" and "Dine'é." The information in this section is based on a number of sources. Among these, the following were particularly helpful: Garrick Bailey and Roberta Glenn Bailey, *A History of the Navajos, The Reservation Years* (Santa Fe: School of American Research Press, 1986); Florence H. Ellis, *Navajo Indians I: An Anthropological Study of the Navajo Indians* (New York: Garland Publishing, 1974); Peter Iverson, *The Navajo Nation* (Albuquerque: University of New Mexico Press, 1981); Raymond Friday Locke, *The Book of the Navajo* (Los Angeles: Mankind Publishing Company, 1976); Frank McNitt, *The Indian Traders* (Norman: University of Oklahoma Press, 1962); Franc Johnson Newcomb, *Navajo Omens and Taboos* (Santa Fe: Rydal Press, 1940); Nancy C. Parezo, *Navajo Sandpainting from Religious Act to Commercial Art* (Tucson: University of Arizona Press, 1963); Willow Roberts and Stokes Carson, *Twentieth-Century Trading on the Navajo Reservation* (Albuquerque: University of New Mexico Press, 1987); Robert A. Roessel, Jr., *Navajo Arts and Crafts* (Rough Rock, Arizona: Navajo Curriculum Center, 1983); and Alfonso Ortiz, editor, *Southwest*, Vol. 10 of *Handbook of American Indians* (Washington, D.C.: Smithsonian, 1983).

7 For additional information on Yeibichai songs, see David P. McAllester and Douglas F. Mitchell, "Navajo Music." In *Southwest*, Vol. 10 of *Handbook of North American Indians* (Washington: Smithsonian Institution, 1983), 608-610.

8 Several other dealers and writers were important in the process of bringing Navajo pottery to the attention of the broader public: Jan Bell, Curator of Collections at the Arizona State Museum at the University of Arizona in Tucson; Russell Hartman, former Director of the Navajo Tribal Museum (now Navajo Nation Museum) in Window Rock, Arizona; and Jan Musial, a writer/dealer in Flagstaff, Arizona.

9 Adson quotes are part of a display in connection with *Shonto Junction; Where Navajo Potteries Meet*, an exhibition at Arizona State Museum, University of Arizona, Tucson, 1990–1993.

THE EASTERN REGION

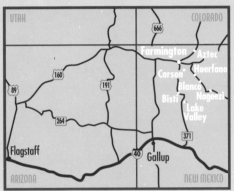

The eastern section of Navajo Country, located entirely in New Mexico, is best explored by driving the three two-lane highways running roughly north and south through the area: New Mexico 44 from Albuquerque to Farmington; 371 (the Vietnam Veterans Highway, completed in the 1960s and paved later) from Thoreau to Farmington; or U.S. 666 between Gallup and Shiprock (the boundary line between our eastern and central regions). When the first Navajo hogan and sheep corral appear nestled in the piñon- and juniper-studded landscape of northern New Mexico, you will know that you have entered the Navajo Nation.

If you ask directions of a Navajo, don't be surprised if the response is in that language. And when you do ask for directions, don't expect to be given street names and numbers. They do not exist in dirt-track Indian country. Art Vigil, a famous Pueblo potter and our neighbor in Tesuque, told us that street names and numbers caused only confusion. "I know where everyone lives," he said. "Every family has its place. Why should we clutter up the pueblo with unnecessary signs and numbers?"

Above: The sign and mural at the historic Nageezi Trading Post were painted by Lawrence Jacquaz, pictured. Opposite: Elizabeth Willeto Ignacio, *Woman*, c. 1989. Painted and carved wood, 9 1/2" x 3 1/2" x 1 1/2".

One of the first stops on New Mexico 44 is the historic, low-slung, wooden-sided trading post at Nageezi. The present sign and mural on the post facade were painted by Lawrence Jacquaz, one of the artists featured in this section. A large American flag flies from a pole at least twenty feet above the roof of the post, which sits on a hill facing the road. There is an island of gas pumps in the parking lot filled with ever-present pickup trucks. You won't miss it.

One of the original sections of the post, nestled under a cluster of old, gnarled cottonwood trees, has been recently remodeled and turned into an inviting bed and breakfast inn. There is little else at Nageezi except a cluster of about thirty brown-stuccoed houses. Lawrence and Luann Jacquaz live in one of these newly built houses south of the post. "After our marriage, we had to live in our family hogan," Luann Murphy Jacquaz explained. "We waited for two long years for the Navajo Housing Authority to make our present home available."

We first stopped at Nageezi in the spring of 1985, looking for the hogan of the Willeto family. This was our first experience at trying to find the camp of a Navajo. Trader Harry Batchelor, whose son, Don, now manages the post and handles some contemporary Navajo folk art, knew the approximate location of the hogan. The Willeto family had been customers for many years. However, the trader had never ventured up the steep walls of the canyon west of Nageezi to visit the Willetos. Fortunately, a Navajo woman who worked for Batchelor was able to draw us a map.

The map was on a brown paper bag, with X's, circles, and squares for fences, sheep camps, and hogans. Washes were indicated by wavy ink scratches, but dirt tracks were not really shown. At one point on our journey, I stopped in the middle of a dry wash in

frustration. "Jan!" I must admit I barked, "Left or right?" "Here's the map," she said. "Decide for yourself!" The effort was worth it in the end. We were the first Anglos to visit the Willetos, and they were genuinely pleased to meet us.

Charlie Willeto's innovative carvings were actually preserved through an amazing chain of events, which illustrates the influence of Indian traders in this field. Nageezi was the closest post to the Willeto hogan, but Harry Batchelor, the trader/postmaster there, was not interested in these carvings, so Willeto brought them instead to the post at Lybrook.

Nageezi and Lybrook, ten miles to the southeast, are virtual look-alikes. Both still cater to the everyday needs of the Navajos, selling yard goods, food, fodder, and hardware. Lybrook was named after its original founder, Bill Lybrook, nephew of the tobacco heir R.J. Reynolds. Jim Mauzy, the trader at Lybrook in the 1960s, was willing to exchange small amounts of foodstuffs for Charlie Willeto's carvings even though they appeared strange to him.

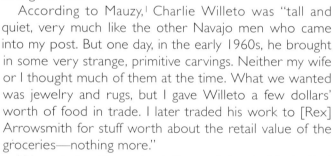

Left: Charlie Willeto, *Two Navajo Men*, c. 1960. Pine board with house paint, 28" x 13" x 10" and 28 3/4" x 5" x 4".

According to Mauzy,[1] Charlie Willeto was "tall and quiet, very much like the other Navajo men who came into my post. But one day, in the early 1960s, he brought in some very strange, primitive carvings. Neither my wife or I thought much of them at the time. What we wanted was jewelry and rugs, but I gave Willeto a few dollars' worth of food in trade. I later traded his work to [Rex] Arrowsmith for stuff worth about the retail value of the groceries—nothing more."

Although Jim Mauzy took the sculptural objects that Willeto brought into his store, he personally did not feel that they had great value. Mauzy was really looking for silver jewelry, a commodity in which he traded most of his life. He owned turquoise mines in Arizona, sold these blue semiprecious gems to Native Americans, and wholesaled their finished jewelry.

The next link in the chain that eventually brought Charlie Willeto's work to the forefront was Rex Arrowsmith (born 1925), an Indian trader willing to take risks on almost anything that is Indian made. Rex Arrowsmith started out, in 1948, as a mining engineer in Arizona, but soon he was trading with the Navajo "on the side."

By 1959, Arrowsmith had opened a trading post, bearing his name, on the old Santa Fe Trail in Santa Fe. "One day at Lybrook, in the early 1960s, Mauzy showed me these strange carved figures—men with foreshortened arms, owls, and other animals. No Navajo had ever made anything like them. I traded Jim and took 'em to Santa Fe."

Arrowsmith didn't know what to make of the carvings, and today he's not even sure he owns one. But, according to Arrowsmith, about four hundred went through his hands during the 1960s. "I sold the medium-sized works for between ten and fifteen dollars," Arrowsmith recalls. Today, these works sell for five thousand dollars and up.

The New York collector and author Herbert Waide Hemphill, Jr. [2] was the next link in the chain. Hemphill bought two of Willeto's full-sized standing figures that at one time had been left to weather outside of Jim Mauzy's trading post in Lybrook. Hemphill bought them from a Santa Fe dealer who had, in turn, acquired them from Rex Arrowsmith. Hemphill's purchase was made while he was on a collecting trip to New Mexico in 1977. He took the figures home with him to New York, and they were later acquired by the Smithsonian's National Museum of American Art by gift and purchase in 1986. The chain from Nageezi to Washington, D.C. was now complete.

The chain of discovery for much of the contemporary Navajo folk art found in the eastern region begins at Farmington, New Mexico, a short drive north of Nageezi. Farmington, with its nearby oil and gas fields, has the bustle and color of a present-day frontier town. Native Americans come here to pawn jewelry, sell livestock, shop, and find employment.

Farmington, on the northern bank of the San Juan River, is just off the reservation. It is also a gateway to the Navajo Nation. U.S. 64 and 160 are the only through paved east-west-northern routes for tourists on their way to such destinations as Monument Valley and Grand Canyon. U.S. 160 turns north into Colorado at Teec Nos Pos, where it also intersects U.S. 64, which runs west from Farmington.

Our folk art adventures often started in Farmington because Indian trader Jack Beasley lives there. Beasley sold his Farmington gallery in 1993, opening Beasley Trading under the management of his son, Jason, in Sedona, Arizona. He continues to reside in Farmington, however, and buys and sells Navajo folk art from his home there.

Beasley is the beginning link in the chain of discovery for much of the contemporary folk art of the eastern and central regions of the Dinétah. This resourceful trader has promoted Navajo art from coast to coast. In December of 1990, for instance, the Museum of American Folk Art invited Jack Beasley to lecture in New York at the Cultural Center. At the appointed time, Beasley approached the lectern wearing his large, museum-quality sandcast silver belt buckle from the 1890s, western hat, boots, and assorted turquoise. Nonchalantly, he spread out on the stage Mamie Deschillie's cutouts, several Hathale muslins, and Johnson Antonio's carvings. His audience, some of the most sophisticated collectors in the country, left their seats with checkbooks in hand.

Trader Jack Beasley was one of the first to recognize the importance of Navajo folk art.

But this sort of art-world acclaim did not come overnight to Beasley, who was born in 1941. He learned the business of the Indian trader slowly and from the bottom up. "During the turquoise boom of 1975," Beasley explained, "I started out buying jewelry 'out of pawn' and selling it to stores and galleries in larger cities. In 1978, I went into business with one of the Mannings [an old Indian trading family] and operated Beasley-Manning Trading Company in Farmington. We loaned on 'pawn,' sold craft items to Indians, retailed Navajo jewelry to Anglos and Indians alike, and wholesaled throughout the Southwest."

Beasley bought out his partner in 1989 and gave up the pawn business. "The great 'old pawn' was mostly gone by then," he said, "but I knew the Indians and believed in their art and the possibility of making a success in the gallery business."

By 1989, Jack Beasley and his wife, Judy, were thoroughly established in the gallery business in Farmington. They had been collecting antiques for their home since 1960—and Navajo folk art since 1983. "I didn't know what to call it," Beasley recently said, "but a great piece of folk art will just stand out every time. The first Navajo folk art I remember seeing was one small mud toy by Elsie Benally—a noseless Navajo woman, dressed in bits of cloth, on a sun-fired clay horse. The piece was less than five inches in height. She brought it to me in 1983, and I said 'go make me more of these,' and that started the whole thing."

During the Christmas season of 1983, while on a house-hunting trip to Santa Fe, we saw a small display of mud toys by Elsie Benally and Mamie Deschillie and some carvings by Johnson Antonio. They had been supplied by Beasley to the Wheelwright Museum of the American Indian. We knew what to call these delightful objects—contemporary Navajo folk art.

The truck-clogged southern arterial that allows access to the Navajo Nation is U.S. 40—Grants, Thoreau, Gallup, Holbrook, and Winslow are all on this route. For the person with time

Mamie Deschillie, *Creche*, 1985. Mixed media (sun-dried clay, cloth, and found objects), figures range in height from 1" to 5".

to explore, there are trading posts, pawn shops, art galleries, westernwear stores, and just plain tourist stops. There are great finds in "old pawn" and Native American art in colorful surroundings, but in many of these shops you have to know what you are about. It is illegal in Arizona and New Mexico to sell merchandise as "Indian made" if it is not, but quality is an elusive matter involving personal choice.

Exit U.S. 40 at Thoreau, and New Mexico 371 north toward Farmington will take you through the center of our eastern region. This is a beautiful drive through a sparsely populated area on the Navajo Nation. The drive winds through semi-mountainous red mesa country studded with piñon and juniper and traverses high deserts punctuated by moonscape rock formations. Distant storm clouds, lightning, and dust storms can enhance the excitement of the moment. A few miles to the west is Chaco Culture National Historic Park. Its Anasazi ruins are an important tourist and camping attraction.

Crownpoint is the only town of any size on this route. The rest of the dots on the map indicate trading posts, Navajo chapter houses, and small clusters of homes. Crownpoint is the area's center of commerce, and there are convenience stores, a medical clinic, and most of the other businesses and services that are present in rural America.

Crownpoint is also where the price of contemporary Navajo rugs is set at frequent late-night auctions in the local elementary school gymnasium. The rug auctions, usually held on the last Friday of the month, are extremely colorful affairs. The Navajo weavers bring in their ware early in the evening and then sit patiently for hours on folding chairs arranged around the outside perimeters of the large, high-ceilinged basketball court waiting for the results of the sale. The women dress in their finest velvet and turquoise and wrap themselves in decorative trade blankets and shawls against the chill of evening. Traders, dealers, pickers, and occasional tourists (anyone is welcome) set up their folding chairs in the center of the room or wander in and out, inspecting the rugs piled on tables at the back of the gym. The rugs sold at auction in Crownpoint will later be retailed in stores throughout the country.

Between Crownpoint and Bloomfield to the north, there are virtually no trees, little grass, and no water—except when rain causes the washes to spew out dangerous torrents. This area, north and west of Lake Valley, is often referred to as the Bisti (the actual Bisti is a wilderness area, 3,946 acres of scenic badlands, protected by an act of Congress in 1984).

The Trading Post at Tsaya sits atop a small nob of a hill and is highly visible when approached from the north or south. The Navajo in the region translate *Tsaya* as "Water Under the Rock." We questioned some elderly women shopping at Tsaya. They remembered an earlier post, located farther to the east, where there really was water under the rock.

Right: Florence Riggs, *Dinosaurs*, c. 1991 (Pre - *Jurassic Park)*. Pictorial rug, commercial yarn, 44" x 51". Photograph by Jerry Sinkovec.

There are usually a number of pickup trucks parked outside because it is the most convenient remaining post for the Navajo in this area. It is a brick two-story structure, parallel to the highway, one of those unmarked posts that can only be identified by the two old gas pumps standing sentinel outside. Tsaya Trading Post has been in the Ashcroft family since about 1942, and if either of the Ashcrofts—Karl or his son, Ross—are present, they can give rough directions to the home of the Navajo artists who are also their customers, though they themselves do not venture out to visit them.

The Ashcrofts do not display rugs or folk art. Their business is strictly the sale of commodities (including yarn) to the Navajos. The interior of Tsaya is a shelf-lined, no-nonsense, old-fashioned store, stocked with convenience foods and staples—potatoes, flour, salt, and food for livestock. This is the gateway to Sandy and Bob Beyale, Johnson Antonio, and Sheila Antonio, an interesting stop on a journey to or from Farmington. But finding the artists isn't always that easy.

Lorena Antonio had printed "JOHNSON ANTONIO" and a post office box number in Kirtland, New Mexico, on the base of sculptures we purchased from Indian trader Jack Beasley in 1984 and 1985. When the Antonios didn't answer our many letters, we drove to Kirtland 60 miles to the north of Lake Valley to look for them. To our surprise, the

postmaster at Kirtland did not know Johnson Antonio either. Antonio was following an established custom (one with which we were not familiar at the time)—using a trader's post office box and picking up his mail, after it had been collected by the trader, at a post near his home.

For two days, we drove in circles south of Kirtland, asking as we went. Finally, we learned that the Antonios actually lived in Lake Valley. Once we knew that, the Ashcrofts at Tsaya Trading Post gave us fairly good directions to their home, which is on a dirt road several miles from the highway. This adventure was repeated time and time again as we sought out artists whose work had intrigued us.

Right: Robin Willeto, *Three-Headed Skinwalker*, 1991. Carved and painted wood, 36 1/2" x 20" x 9 1/2".

Johnson Antonio

In the 1990s, images of Johnson Antonio's dolls have appeared in newspapers and magazines across the country, and he has received favorable reviews wherever his art has been shown. When we first met this artist in 1985, he was driving a horse-drawn wagon. Today, he rides in a blue shag–carpeted Chevy van, large enough for his family of eight children. He is the most successful of the Navajo carvers and an important role model for younger artists.

But the art of Johnson Antonio was a long time in developing, and it is created in an unlikely place—a barren and impoverished corner of northwestern New Mexico called the Bisti. Antonio was born in Lake Valley near the trading post called Tsaya in 1931. He attended the Lake Valley School off and on until 1949.

Opposite: Johnson Antonio, *Embracing Couple,* c. 1990. Acrylic on carved cottonwood, 13 1/4" x 3" x 3".

In 1951, Antonio went to work for the Union Pacific Railroad. "They picked me up in a bus at the trading post," he remembers, "and took me off to lay steel. It was hard work, and when the laying was done in the fall, they'd take me home again. I'd collect unemployment till they'd come for me in the spring. In 1974, I decided I didn't want to go anymore." Antonio returned home for good and began herding sheep and goats.

While he was away from home working for the Union Pacific, Antonio married Lorena Henry by correspondence. The family currently lives in a home they built themselves on the edge of a deep wash almost twenty years ago. "It's wearing down," Johnson recently said, referring to his paint-faded, tar-and-shingle–roofed dwelling, "I'm trying to get some money from the Navajo Housing Authority to build it up again."

There is no wood suitable for carving on the Bisti. But the compulsion to make art can appear in the most unlikely of places. When Antonio was over fifty years of age (late 1982 or early 1983), he found some cottonwood in a wash near Farmington, took it home, and "just began." He roughs the figure out with an ax and finishes the details with a pocket knife. The finished work is not sanded, but it is painted with watercolor. Recently, Lorena Antonio has been doing some of the painting, using acrylics in addition to watercolors. Most of the whites in the early pieces are *dleesh* (a clay used by the Navajos to paint their bodies for ceremonies).

Dleesh, however, is a very fragile pigment easily rubbed off or dissolved by water.

The artist is unable to describe with words his initial creative impulse: "They come from here," he says, pointing to his heart. And later, he thought, "Maybe—just maybe" somebody would give him needed dollars for his work. On a second impulse, he made the forty-mile trip to Farmington and showed his carvings to Indian trader Jack Beasley. Antonio's link to the art world was established.

The Hopi refer to kachina carvings as "dolls," and when the Navajo carve kachinas, they too refer to them in this manner. Antonio also calls his carvings dolls, but they are not playtoys; nor are they intended to be used as ceremonial objects. Antonio carves what he knows best—sculptural likenesses of the Diné. His dolls are dressed for the climate as the Navajo have dressed for the last hundred years—in jeans, trade blankets, and velvet; they lean into the wind, covering their heads against cold, heat, and dust. The harshness of survival is etched into their faces and mirrored in their posture. (Antonio, with the help of his wife Lorena, also made sheep and goats with real fur and horns in the early- to mid-1980s. When the Grawlers started to make similar animals, their early carvings were sometimes attributed to Antonio. Presently, several other families are making animals; these are attributed to Ray Growler in some instances.) Johnson Antonio carves for the money, but he also carves out of a desire to communicate with the outside world—a world he is slowly discovering. As he puts it: "I make them for myself, but I need the money. Unfortunately, the cash will soon be gone, but the dolls will live forever."

Antonio's carvings have been widely exhibited and were included in a touring exhibition sponsored by the Museum of American Folk Art in New York City. They are in the permanent collection of the Museum of American Folk Art, the Smithsonian Institution's National Museum of American Art in Washington, D.C., and the Wheelwright Museum of the American Indian in Santa Fe.

Johnson Antonio,
Rabbit Hunter, 1986.
Watercolor and pencil on carved
cottonwood, 19" x 6" x 3 1/2".

Sheila Antonio

Sheila Antonio (no relation to Johnson Antonio) captures humorous moments in Navajo life in tiny, beaded sculptures. She was born in the Bisti on March 27, 1961, and she went to the boarding school at Toadlena, completing the eleventh grade at Farmington High School.

Antonio explains how her obsession with this eye-straining art form came about: "In grade school, they taught us to make belts, watch fobs, and headbands—things good little Indian girls should make from beads as family gifts. But I knew that beadwork could be more than pretty trinkets, and so I figured out my own style."

Every trading post keeps large jars and boxes of beads sold by weight, but the Navajo are not particularly known for fine decorative beadwork. Most of the beads are strung into necklaces or used for decoration on tourist items or clothing.

Right: Sheila Antonio, *Weaving While Children Play*, 1992. Beadwork (glass beads over metal armature on leather base), 2 ¹/₂" x 2" x 2".

What Antonio did was "find these metal things used in electric circuits" to form armatures for her sculptures. "With them, super-glue, and cotton stuffing, I can build horses, cows, or hogans—anything. I string my beads and cover the forms so that the whole thing looks like beadwork."

Sheila Antonio's sense of humor catches the disappearing Navajo way of life in a contemporary style. Her colorful sculptures, often no more than two inches in height, have been exhibited at the Wheelwright Museum of the American Indian, and her work may be seen in many galleries.

Sandy Beyale

Five dirt-track miles from the post at Tsaya, on a rise over-looking a broad, rocky wash, there's an encampment of four or five black plywood hogans—the extended Beyale family's home. A basketball hoop is affixed to the west side of one of the hogans, and a game is usually in progress. The plywood of the hogan forms a perfect backboard, and since the structure's only window faces east, kids can safely play without fear of breaking glass.

Deep in the wash there are cauldronlike holes in the bedrock where greenish, sun-warmed, algae-stained water survives, enough for cattle throughout the heat of summer. Drinking water for the Beyales is trucked from Bloomfield and stored in metal barrels on the lip of the wash. This is the Bisti, and there is precious little grass for the twenty sheep and goats and four horses upon which the family of two adults and seven boys depends.

Sandy Beyale was born here in 1971 and attended high school at Crownpoint. "I would have liked to have found a job near home," he explains, "but there are none. So in summer I work in Salt Lake City as a welder's helper. But this summer [1992], I enlisted in the Army and have to report to Oklahoma, come September."

Sandy Beyale started carving representations of Navajo men and women at the suggestion of his mother, Lillian Beyale, in 1987. Beyale explains his adventure into art this way: "Mother went into Farmington to check on [cash a check at] Beasley [Beasley-Manning Trading Post] and saw the carvings of Johnson Antonio on display. She came home and said, 'you can do that too.'" Antonio is a "clan brother" of Beyale's; they both belong to the *Kiiyaa' áanii* (Towering Rock) clan. The Beyale and Antonio children often ride their horses across the rocky wash to exchange visits. But business

‹ Left: Sandy Beyale, *Navajo Woman with Pepsi,* 1990. Carved and painted wood, 8 1/2" x 2 1/4" x 2 3/4".

36

is business, and Beyale did not know that his clan brother was selling sculpture through Beasley until his mother saw the display in Farmington. "So," Beyale says, "I thought about how it would be if the past were now—men still had their hair tied in buns—and began carving the people I knew."

Beyale carves from cottonwood and paints with brightly colored, unmixed acrylics. His representations of the People from the past, with their hair in buns, are drinking from Pepsi cans and are otherwise engaged in contemporary activities. There is humor in this work, and Beyale's depiction of smooth, unwrinkled faces containing white, diamond-shaped eyes with small black pupils set him apart from other Navajo carvers.

The artist is proud of the fact that he taught his father, Bob Beyale, to carve. The senior Beyale retired after working many summers away from home as a laborer for the Union Pacific and Southern Pacific railroads. He differentiates his work from that of his son as follows: "I make and sign mine. He makes and signs his." In truth, the sculpture of the two carvers is hard to tell apart, so the signatures are convenient. Sandy Beyale's touch appears to be the lighter of the two and his sense of humor more pronounced.

Father and son sell their work through Bill Foutz's Trading Post in Shiprock. "I guess I've wholesaled more than a hundred of their carvings," Foutz proudly explains. "I don't know what the relationship is between Sandy and Bob and don't care who makes what. I will buy all I can get!"

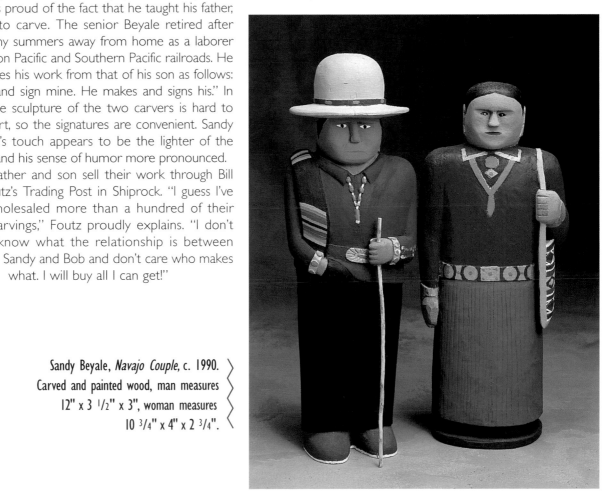

Sandy Beyale, *Navajo Couple,* c. 1990. Carved and painted wood, man measures 12" x 3 1/2" x 3", woman measures 10 3/4" x 4" x 2 3/4".

37

Delbert Buck

Night and day, there's the chunk, chunk, chunk in the air from machinery pumping oil and gas under Navajoland and a swish, swish from the huge arms of irrigation equipment spraying water onto the fields of the federally sponsored Navajo Indian Irrigation Project. But none of this newly created wealth has rubbed off on the nearby Bucks, who live in Gallegos Wash, located a few miles north of the historic Carson Trading Post near Farmington and Bloomfield, New Mexico.

Left: Delbert Buck, *Motorcycle Rider,* 1990. Carved and painted wood, 31" x 15" x 5 ½".

The Buck family members are typical Navajo herders of sheep and goats.

Besides Wilford Buck and his wife, Jennie, a weaver, there are eight children (two boys and six girls).

One of these children, Delbert Buck, was born in 1976 and presently attends high school in Bloomfield. He is the youngest folk artist we know. Buck started making sculpture from found objects at age twelve, which isn't uncommon, but he achieved representation in commercial galleries by age fourteen, which is. "The ideas just keep coming," he recently explained. "I see things all around me and just make them out."

Delbert Buck assembles constructions from found objects and combines them with crudely carved and painted figures. Humor and satire are central to his art. Buck's sculptures often make fun of politicians. In one assemblage, for instance, a donkey wearing Nikes is racing a tortoise wearing a sort-of Uncle Sam hat. In other works, his Navajo neighbors, colorfully decked out, are riding horses or depicted on motorcycles.

The family gives Delbert Buck all of the credit, but he does get considerable assistance from others, especially his father and his older sister, Emma. We tried to determine exactly who did what and pretty definitely established that Wilford helped with the carving and painting and that Emma often decorates and dresses the figures and helps paint the work.

Collectively, the Buck family takes great pride in these humorous works. In fact, in our most recent visit with family members, we learned that two of Delbert's brothers (Philbert and Larry) are beginning to take an interest in Delbert's folk art enterprise. They are starting to help with the assembling, dressing, and painting of the objects and are even making a few pieces of their own. While Buck is prolific, the work is often interrupted for long periods of time for family ventures such as summer work picking potatoes in Colorado.

Wilford Buck introduced his son to Jack Beasley in 1988, and Beasley has been promoting the artist throughout the Southwest. Delbert Buck has been featured at the Leslie Muth Gallery in Santa Fe, as well as other galleries showing contemporary folk art.

Delbert Buck, *Buffalo Rider*, 1991. Carved and painted wood, lamb's wool, and leather, 31" x 26" x 8".

Matilda Damon

"I wanted to experience something different—something no one else could make—so I started weaving round pictorials in 1988," Matilda Damon said. "It's a secret [how to build a round loom]. If you give my secret away, everybody will make them."

Damon, who was born in 1962, grew up in a log cabin near Ganado, Arizona, where the famous Hubbell Trading Post is located. "My father took care of the sheep," she remembers, "and Mother [Mary Damon] wove large rugs [4' by 8' to 6' by 10'] mostly in the happiness design." Matilda Damon has incorporated chains of arrowheads near the left and right borders of her pictorial rug. These chains are the principal element of her mother's happiness design.

Matilda Damon explains that she "didn't get much school, but a few years ago, I got a GED at the San Juan College in Farmington, and I am currently taking some general courses at the college. Maybe I'll become a lab technician or a teacher."

Mary Damon taught her daughter to weave when she was about ten years old. "At first," Matilda Damon says, "I made small rugs, about 12" by 24". We sold them at Lucero's Trading Post in Window Rock. It was a big deal for me because I got to choose some of the groceries that Mother bought with the money— mostly sweets."

Damon moved to Fruitland (an area on the Navajo reservation south of the San Juan River) a few years ago. This move brought her nearer to Farmington and the San Juan College. She has a good-sized family—three girls and one boy. "I'm teaching my

Left: Matilda Damon, *Indian Faces*, 1991. Round pictorial rug, handspun wool, native and vegetable dyes, 21" diameter.
Opposite: *Indian Family*, 1992. Round pictorial rug, handspun and commercial yarn, 26 1/2" diameter.

girls how to weave now," she says with pride. Shaundina Watson (age thirteen) and Shannon Watson (age ten) were both making very attractive and useful round coasters with butterflies. "We sell them at the Foutz Trading Company in Shiprock," Shaundina gleefully exclaims. "And I get to keep my own money!"

Matilda Damon is a meticulous colorist. Her ability to create and use subtle variations of tone is rare in a Navajo weaver. "Most of my wool is given to me at shearing time by relatives and friends," she said. "I dye it with natural mineral and vegetable colors. But I can also spin two or more colors together to create yarn in new shades. For instance, gray is natural white and black spun together, and I can get many variations of the same color. I used different shades of brown [white and natural brown wool] for the eagle than the one I used on the faces of the women in your rug." But, as often happens, when Damon is unable to spin the exact color she is looking for, she buys it at local posts.

Damon says that her ideas come to her while she is out driving or walking. "I see something I want to remember and sketch it out on paper. Later, I go through my idea-sketches looking for the right picture for a rug."

Damon could have spent her life, as her mother did before her, repeating the same patterns over-and-over again. That she has chosen to be creative and make innovative round pictorials sets her apart from most other Navajo weavers.

Mamie Deschillie

Mamie Deschillie is one of the "superstars" of contemporary Navajo folk art.
Wherever her art is shown, young and old alike chuckle out loud, marveling at her
sense of humor and ingenuity. She has added her personal vision to the tradition of
making "mud toys" (figurines of sun-dried earth or clay, originally intended as playtoys

Opposite: Mamie Deschillie, *Nine Cutout Figures,* 1987-91. Mixed media (cardboard, paint, cloth, sequins, beads, and jewelry), figures range in size from 17" x 6" x ¹/₂" to 46" x 15" x 3".

for children), a tradition noted as early as 1881. The practice
apparently died out many years ago, perhaps in the 1940s.[3]
Deschillie's creative stories in mud and cardboard contain elements
of Navajo mannerisms and surroundings; she is an ambassador of
goodwill for the ways and customs of the Diné.

It is very surprising that this sort of accolade would accompany the
biography of a traditional Navajo woman of the older generation.
Deschillie was born on July 27, 1920, in the small, sheep-herding community of Burnham, New Mexico, and did not attend school beyond the second grade. She learned to weave as a child, a practice she continues to this
day. Her skills with a loom have been recognized, but her rugs are far more
traditional than her inventive collages of mud and cardboard.

Deschillie lives in a house trailer parked alongside the prefabricated home of
her son and daughter-in-law in Fruitland, south of the San Juan River near
Farmington. Recently, she has added a boxlike plywood studio onto the side of
her trailer. And there's a brand new sewing machine in the studio to help make
the stitching of discarded cloth onto her cardboard cutouts easier and quicker.

Deschillie is active in community affairs. Among other things, she has been president of the Fruitland Senior Citizens Association. And she loves children! Besides
helping to raise her own grandchildren, Mamie Deschillie does volunteer work accompanying students on school buses. Whenever we came to call on her, Deschillie was
always ready to receive company, dressed in traditional velvet and wearing some of the
finest silver and turquoise we have been privileged to see. She's a beautiful woman.

Strange as it may seem, Deschillie's entry into the art world came about because of
her jewelry. The Navajo can't borrow money on real estate, which is owned in trust
for them by the United States. When money is needed, or sometimes when the
Navajo just want to safeguard possessions, they are pawned. Jack Beasley had a long-
standing business relationship with Deschillie in this regard.

"She was pawning and redeeming beautiful old jewelry right along," Beasley explained. "One day, early in 1983, I asked her if she could bring in something she remembered from childhood. I had made the same request of Elsie Benally and others. Both women, independently, as far as I could determine, brought in mud toys. Elsie was the first, but Mamie's arrived a few days later. I was surprised, but I knew instantly that they were great!"

The mud toys came first. The earth in the Fruitland area was not right for fashioning the toys Deschillie remembered from her childhood, and so she had her daughter-in-law drive her to Burnham (the place of her birth) to dig her raw material. She formed the "toys" out of a combination of earth and water and fired them in the hot New Mexico sun on a wooden table in the backyard. Today, the mud figures are dressed in bits of cloth, colored paper, beads, spangles, turquoise, fur, and just about anything else you can imagine. Watercolors are also used to add realism and further enhance the creative designs. Once Deschillie was launched on her new career, her imagination took over. Her subject matter ranges from familiar field animals to the esoteric—cowboys riding roosters and circus animals she has seen only in illustrated children's books.

Opposite: Mamie Deschillie, *Goat,* 1985. Mixed media (cardboard, pencil, and goat's wool), 29" x 37".

In the mid-1980s, Mamie Deschillie began making fanciful collages that were different from anything else that had ever been made by a Navajo, and that break new ground as an art form. She calls this work "cardboards" or "cutouts" because the basic material is cardboard—boxes saved from the dumpster. She cuts the raw material into the desired shape with a pair of ordinary household scissors. The cutouts are brought to life by collaged material applied to the surface—discarded long johns, fur, sequins—the same sort of flotsam and jetsam that she used for the earlier mud toys. This use of discarded material is audience pleasing. When museum viewers realize that they are looking at what may have been discarded underwear, grins universally appear, and the silence of hushed galleries is interrupted by laughter. Although the subject matter of Deschillie's two art forms is similar, the principal difference is that the cutouts are much larger (ranging upwards to five feet in height), and they are not as fragile as the sun-dried mud toys, which have to be handled with extreme care.

Two of Mamie Deschillie's cutouts have toured the country in an exhibition sponsored by the Museum of American Folk Art in New York City. In 1993, Deschillie was one of the American folk artists included in an exhibition at the Collection de l'art brut in Lausanne, Switzerland. A Deschillie mud toy toured throughout the nation in an exhibition sponsored by the American Federation of the Arts, *Lost and Found Traditions: Native American Art 1965-1985.* Her work is in numerous public and private collections.

Lawrence Jacquaz

In an early morning dream, Lawrence Jacquaz (pronounced Hackus) had a vision of "a little boy sitting high on *Dził Ná'oodiłii* ["Mountain Around Which Moving Was Done," referred to by the Navajo as "twirling mountain'"] and mistlike, sunburst-horned Yeibichai floating up into the sky." He told us that at first light, when he tried to paint his dream, "a carving came out."

Opposite: Lawrence Jacquaz, *Corn Pollen, Nightway Chant*, 1991. Mixed media (wood, colored sand, and acrylic paint, mounted on a stone base), 28" x 25" x 3".

Lawrence Jacquaz was born in 1965. His early years were spent in a hogan under the shadow of Dził Ná'oodiłii. "There is an old cedar hogan weathering away near the top of the mountain," he says. "I believe that First Man and First Woman may have lived there." (According to the Navajo origin legend, First Man and First Woman were the first beings to appear as humans; they formed the four mountains sacred to the Navajo from soil gathered from mountains in the prior world. Their legendary home was located near Huerfano Mountain.)

After finishing about eight grades in a boarding school, Jacquaz worked part-time for Foutz and Burson Construction Company. In 1988, a jackhammer accident ended this short career. Jacquaz now lives with his wife, Luann Murphy Jacquaz, in a small village of houses just south of the Nageezi Trading Post. "I had been painting off and on all my life," he remembers, "but after my dream I started to carve."

The work of Lawrence Jacquaz is unique among Navajo artists. He has created a style of art that relates to both sandpainting and sculpture. His negative spaces give the art a three-dimensional form. Jacquaz sculpts cutout, free-standing constructions and wall plaques. Intricate colorful Navajo designs and Yei figures are assembled and glued puzzlelike to boards, forming an open-faced picture composed largely of personal symbols that only the artist can translate. One figure that appears frequently is the Sunburst Yei, Chiricahua Apache, which is found in Navajo legend. The artist says that he's unable "to duplicate the figures and the colors exactly" because in the Navajo religion "that would be wrong." Like many other Navajos, Jacquaz believes that a complete and accurate rendering of sacred designs would imbue the object with supernatural power, inappropriate for secular use. Thus, as many artists change the details of

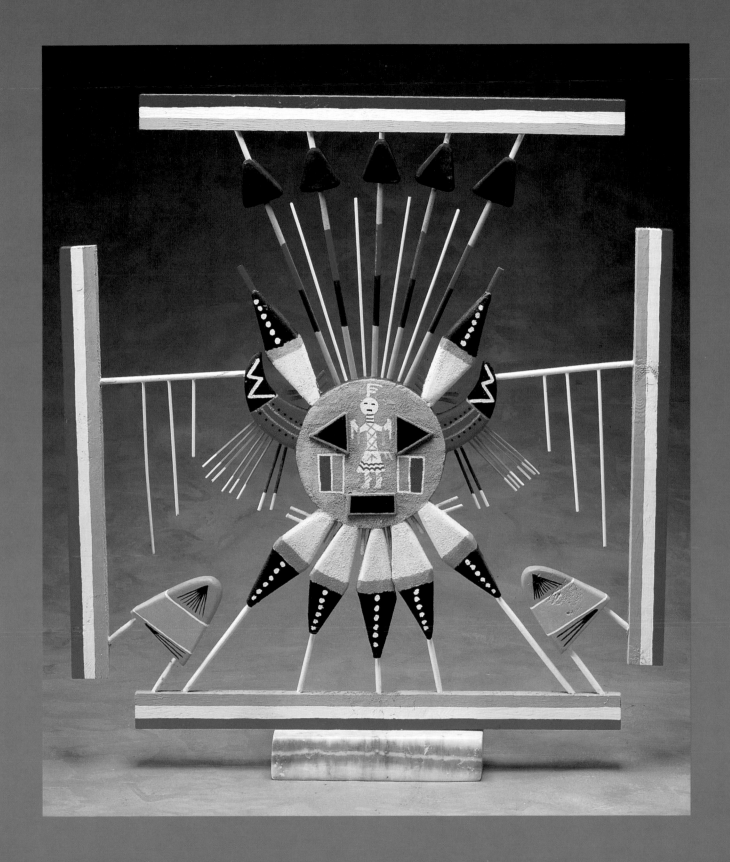

sandpaintings to prevent the Holy People from being called, so Jacquaz alters the designs he relies on in creating his sculptures.

Lawrence Jacquaz also continues to paint. For instance, he recently completed several large murals, one on the outside wall of the Nageezi Trading Post and another on the side of a nearby barn facing the highway. These murals of Navajo scenes, while interesting, lack the personal vision and innovation that is present in the carvings, and the painted works are not collected with the same enthusiasm as his carvings.

His wood pieces are painted with a mixture of the sand "medicine men use," held together by Elmer's Glue, and commercial oil paints to achieve colors "I can't get right with sand." Luann Jacquaz helps with the painting.

In the spring of 1989, Jacquaz brought his first few pieces to Don Batchelor at the Nageezi Trading Post. Impressed, the trader both personally collected the sculpture and offered works for sale to the occasional tourist. Shortly thereafter, Bruce Burns, owner of the Thomas Harley Trading Post in Aztec, began to represent this innovative artist and has placed his work in important collections.

Lawrence Jacquaz, *The Four Houses of the Sun,* 1990. Mixed media (wood, colored sand, and acrylic paint), 45 ¹/₂" x 46 ¹/₂".

The Pete Sisters

Fannie Pete, who was born in Gallegos Canyon near Bloomfield on February 10, 1958, is one of the most imaginative contemporary pictorial weavers. Her younger sister, Julia Pete, is also an innovative weaver. Because Julia started weaving after her sister's work was well known, however, her rugs do not generally command as high a price as those of Fannie.

The Pete sisters learned weaving from their mother, Bessie Pete, who was making bead earrings for the tourist market on the day of our first visit. According to Fannie Pete, "Mother used to bring her rugs into Carson's, but Jo [Jo Carson Drolet] is gone, and the new owners don't buy rugs. Mother made some animals once in a while, but not like mine."

The loss of their traditional market at Carson's discouraged Fannie Pete. "My sister-in-law kept telling me: 'you'd better get a job in Farmington,' but I like it here. I help on the farm with the raising of a hundred sheep and sixty goats. We shear them, wash the wool, comb it out, make the dyes from rock and vegetables, and spin it."

Both sisters work on a loom their mother made years ago, set up Navajo style against a wall in their modified hogan that retains the traditional hard-packed dirt floor. (A Navajo woman customarily kneels on the ground in front of a vertical loom.) These two break tradition from time to time. "If we can't get the dye for the right color," Julia Pete explains with guilt in her voice, "we buy the yarn." And Fannie adds, "When I get tired, I use store-bought from K-Mart or Wal-Mart."

They break tradition in other aspects of their work, as well, by creating new and innovative designs. "It's easy to make a rug from a pattern supplied by a trader, and I have done it on order," Fannie Pete explains, "but what I feel I must do is make rugs from my imagination—rugs that have never been made before. If I want to make a green leprechaun, or a white Statue of Liberty, or a blue cow, I weave it."

Fannie Pete can stay at home now because she has found a market for her rugs after all. The Foutz Indian Room, Jack Beasley in Farmington, and the Leslie Muth Gallery in Santa Fe can sell them as fast as they come in the door. But don't be confused; collectors of Navajo rugs are probably not going to buy a Pete. These rugs are being collected by folk art enthusiasts who believe that you cannot make a work of art by simply copying that which has been done before.

Left: Fannie Pete, *Pig*, c. 1987.
Pictorial rug, handspun wool,
native and vegetable dyes,
32" x 27".
Right: Julia Pete, *Red Horse*, c. 1991.
Pictorial rug, commercial yarn,
25 $^1/_2$" x 22 $^1/_2$".

Dennis Pioche

Dennis Pioche is representative of a younger generation of Navajo folk artists who have begun to realize that there is the possibility of forging a career out of their art. But for the present, he lives in Aztec, New Mexico, and works for San Juan County on a road-paving crew. Pioche was born in 1965 in the Blanco Canyon area south of Bloomfield, New Mexico. His father is Navajo and his mother half Navajo, half Sioux. "My father had a job on the Sioux reservation," he explains, "where I attended the Pine Ridge High school in South Dakota, run by the Bureau of Indian Affairs."

But Pioche's formative years were spent on the Navajo Nation learning the Navajo Way. "I mostly stick with the Navajo religion. When I was 16 or 17, I danced in my first Yeibichai ceremony," he says. "It was at Lake Valley, and the ground was deep in snow. Not enough men showed up, so I was enlisted."

Pioche started carving at age two, and by the time he was four years old, he was making his own toys—"mostly cars and things" those days, as he remembers. "Later, I was influenced by my grandfather, John Begay. Grandfather made small, barely roughed-out, stick-like figures from cottonwood roots, which were painted with natural pigments. At the conclusion of a healing ceremony, these primitive carvings were placed behind the east side of a cactus and left there to be destroyed by the elements. The face of the figure pointed eastward, directed toward the sunrise."

Around 1986, Pioche started carving seriously. Pioche's work is relatively small in size and depicts the stoic Navajo in everyday dress—wrapped in trade blankets, for example, standing patiently while waiting for some unexplained event. If you visit any trading post in the Navajo nation, you will recognize a Pioche-like person. The artist also paints stylized versions of Navajo Yeibichai and reservation scenes, but we believe these are not as original as his carvings.

Dennis Pioche carves from cottonwood he finds in the washes near Farmington. To obtain the soft colors he favors, Pioche paints his carvings with watercolors or acrylics mixed with water. His whites are dleesh (or kaolin clay) used as body paint in Navajo ceremonies.

Pioche sells his work through Bruce Burns, who runs the Thomas Harley Trading Post in Aztec. Pioche also exhibits at various fairs and powwows, and this young artist has already had a one-person show at the Los Pinos Trading Company in Durango, Colorado.

Right: Dennis Pioche, *Navajo Man and Woman Wearing Pendleton Blankets*, 1992. Carved cottonwood and acrylic paint with cloth headband, woman measures 16 1/2" x 4" x 3", man measures 14 1/2" x 3 1/2" x 2 3/4".

Dennis Pioche, *Navajo Man Wrapped in Trade Blanket*, c. 1992. Carved cottonwood and acrylic paint, 10 1/2" x 3 1/2" x 3".

The Willeto Family

Charlie Willeto was born on February 20, 1906.[4] He was a tall man. The top of his head, in the only known family picture, is above the hogan's smoke hole. He would have had to stoop to enter his home. Willeto was a medicine man who herded sheep and goats.

But Charlie Willeto is best known as an artist; he was the first contemporary Navajo folk artist to achieve national recognition. Willeto was included in a traveling exhibition of works from the collection of Herbert Waide Hemphill, Jr., circulated by the Milwaukee Art Museum between 1981 and 1984. Willeto's *Male and Female Navajo Figures* (page 8) were considered among the "crown jewels" of this collection. They were acquired through gift and purchase by the Smithsonian Institution's National Museum of American Art in 1986.

Above: A rare Willeto family photo, c. 1963. Photograph by R. Willeto.
Opposite: Charlie Willeto, *Owl*, c. 1962. Pine board with house paint, 22 1/2" x 12 1/4" x 2 1/2".

Charlie Willeto was the first known Navajo artist to carve fanciful, idiosyncratic figures of men and women, owls, and half-imaginary, half-real animals. In the 1960s, when Willeto worked on his figures, several of which are life-sized, there were very few Navajo who broke the taboo of carving out of wood (see also Tom Yazzie, page 105). Willeto carved representations of Navajo men and women that were dreamlike—part religious, part spiritual—with no definitive characteristics attributable to any particular person or spiritual being. The dreamlike quality of his work may be significant in that the Navajo place great importance in dreams and in their interpretation.

When you look at a Willeto carving, you recognize instantly that the figure is Navajo; the figure may be adorned in a concho belt, wear a trade blanket, and have its hair in a Navajo bun, but its features are otherwise "out of focus." It cannot be a real person, a spirit, or a Yei. Likewise, a Willeto owl (owls can bring bad luck if they visit your home) is not a real owl, but an owl spirit that may be sporting a mustache.

Willeto's life has been shrouded in mystery. He has been exhibited under different names. There is no totally reliable date for his birth, and his family sometimes spells the artist's first name "Charlie" and sometimes "Charley." We believe this confusion is

caused by the fact, as is so often the case, that he was referred to at home by his Navajo name.

Willeto lived a pastoral life, high up in a canyon west of the trading post at Nageezi. From all accounts, his life was similar to that of his neighbors, who also herded sheep and goats. Willeto was a medicine man who, according to his widow, Elizabeth Willeto Ignacio, specialized in the Blessingway Ceremony, a rite emphasizing peace, harmony, and good—and one considered by most commentators, including the Navajo, as central to all ceremonial practice. The Blessingway is not intended for curing disease but rather for attracting good luck, averting misfortune, and inviting positive blessings upon man, his livestock, and his possessions. Elizabeth Willeto Ignacio relates that her husband occasionally used small carvings (not the animals) in his performance of the Blessingway ceremony, but that "no other medicine man used them."

Elizabeth and Charlie Willeto shared their hogan with their family of eight. Of the eight Willeto children, only Robin and Harold are still alive today. We were very fortunate in being able to obtain and copy what is said to be their only family portrait. The picture was taken by one of the sons in about 1963. The family was standing in front of their hogan, which is still used by the boys when they are home, though Elizabeth now lives in another house built on the property.

Charlie Willeto didn't start to carve until about 1961. Once he started, he apparently

pursued his art with a great passion, completing as many as four hundred works between 1961 and his death on December 14, 1964. He carved with a hatchet and common woodworking tools (saws and knives). The sculpture was unsanded, and the old sun-weathered boards were left pretty much as he found them. If nails were present in the wood, he carved around them. The wood he used was second-hand; pine and cedar boards could be found anywhere in the area. He painted the wood with house paint and with paint left unused by road crews or at construction sites. For that reason, the quality of the wood and paint was sometimes poor.

We know that Elizabeth Willeto helped in the making of the art. By some family accounts, she helped shape the figures and did part of the painting. Some of the designs and details that appear on the finished carvings may have been hers; the similarity to work she is now doing under her own name is apparent. Although Charlie Willeto never signed any of his sculptures, his style is very recognizable.

Charlie Willeto received almost no recognition during his life. Today, however, his work is widely known and respected. Besides the traveling exhibition in 1981–1984, Willeto has been exhibited at the Maxwell Museum of Anthropology, the Wheelwright Museum of the American Indian, the Denver Art Museum, and other institutions.

Opposite: Elizabeth Willeto Ignacio, *Figure with Upraised Hands*, 1991. Commercial rug dye on carved cottonwood, 19 1/2" x 6 1/2" x 4".

Elizabeth Willeto Ignacio's figures are more finished and refined than those of her late husband, but the basic forms are nearly the same. She also creates partly imaginary, partly ceremonial representations of her Navajo neighbors. The painted decoration on the wood reminds us of the work of Charlie Willeto, but her designs are more detailed.

Born in 1926, she is a proud woman who appears to spend most of her days now sitting on a bench, leaning against the east side of a hogan—the same hogan that she shared with her first husband, Charlie. She dresses in the traditional costume of the Navajo—pleated velvet skirt and velvet blouse. Once, when we approached her, she was not adorned in silver and turquoise, but before granting us an interview, she had her son Harold fetch her precious possessions from within the hogan.

Although Elizabeth Ignacio helped Charlie Willeto with carving and painting, she has carved very few pieces since her first husband died. Ignacio signs her work now ("I.W."), and that's something her husband never did.

Leonard Willeto lived a short, unhappy life in the family compound west of Nageezi. Born in 1955, he had some schooling, but when Willeto was only about sixteen years old, he was run over by a pickup truck. His injuries ended his schooling and left his face terribly scarred. He never married.

In the 1970s, after the death of his father (1964), and following the accident, Leonard Willeto began to carve. He carved in cottonwood and pine and painted with poster paints—bright reds, oranges, greens, and blues. His work was very different from that of the rest of the family, much smaller in scale and brighter in color. Willeto had two basic styles: he carved non-representational Navajo figures with foreshortened arms raised in prayer, and he made flat, doll-like figures of Indians dressed in imaginary costumes, elaborate headdresses, and chicken feathers.

Leonard Willeto made very few dolls, perhaps no more than a hundred. They were sold by Harry Batchelor, the trader at Nageezi, even though Batchelor did not particularly like them personally and had not handled the work of Charlie Willeto. (Unlike his father, who was not enthusiastic about Navajo folk art, Don Batchelor, the present Nageezi trader, carries works by Elizabeth Willeto Ignacio and Leonard's brothers, Harold and Robin, as well as other contemporary folk artists.)

Willeto's career was tragically ended on August 2, 1984, when he took his own life. Today, his brightly painted dolls, which are in public and private collections, are hard to find on the open market.

Left: Leonard Willeto, *Masked Figure,* 1980. Pine board, poster paint, and chicken feathers, 12 1/2" x 3 3/4" x 2 1/4".

Opposite: Leonard Willeto, *Imaginary Figures,* c. 1980. Pine board, poster paint, and chicken feathers, 16" x 4 3/4" x 3 1/2" and 10" x 4 1/2" x 3".

Harold Willeto was born in 1959, *Robin Willeto* in 1962; they are the only living children of Elizabeth and Charlie Willeto. Both boys completed some high school in Bloomfield.

Harold Willeto initially said that he didn't want to carve, but that their mother, Elizabeth, was putting pressure on him to bring in much-needed income. When we first began to write about the family in 1986, Willeto told us that he felt the source of the Willeto "bad luck" was breaking taboos by making carved figures.

Despite his fears, Harold Willeto was making painted cottonwood and pine sculptures by 1988. A short time thereafter, Robin joined the endeavor. Right now, Robin is the more prolific of the two, partly because Harold has seasonal employment, picking crops in Colorado.

Above: Robin Willeto.
Left: Robin Willeto, *Bear,* 1991. Carved cottonwood stained with commercial rug dye, 49" x 16" x 7".
Opposite: Harold Willeto, *Spirit Figure,* 1989. Carved and painted wood, 52" x 13" x 8".

While there are some similarities between the work of the two brothers, especially in the early works, Harold's pieces tend to be larger (nearly life size) and more solid in feeling. His subject matter, though less innovative than Leonard's or Robin's, is closer to his father's. Harold Willeto makes figures with upraised, short, stubby arms that seem to be lifted in prayer. He paints them with house paint, using delicately executed Navajo designs.

Robin currently is doing very imaginative work, unlike that of any other family members. His carvings come from images he sees in dreams—a skinwalker, a catlike person decorated with an owl design, a three-headed personage, or even a spirit bear. His work not only breaks taboo with regard to carved images; it is also nontraditional in every sense. "I see witch spirits in my dreams," Robin relates. "They have white faces and glaring eyes; I sometimes carve them." On his later works, Robin Willeto has been using a commercial stain designed for rugs.

Fortunately, the brothers sign and date their work (so there can be no mistaking Robin for Harold or vice versa).[5] Even without a signature, the recent work of the two is easy to differentiate, based on the subject matter. Don Batchelor at the Nageezi Trading Post tries to stock contemporary folk art, including the Willetos, for the occasional tourist, and Jack Beasley in Farmington wholesales the brothers' work throughout the Southwest. "I have a waiting list," says Beasley. "The demand for the Willetos is much greater than the supply."

Above: Harold Willeto.
Opposite: Robin Willeto, *Skinwalker with Face of Fox and Owl on Body*, c. 1990. Carved and painted wood, 14 1/2" x 3 1/2" x 4".

Notes to Eastern Region

1 Mauzy died in 1992, but his widow still lives in Bloomfield. We interviewed Mauzy off and on from 1986 to 1987, and we have also had several discussions with Mauzy's widow, Iris.

2 See Lynda Roscoe Hartigan, *Made with Passion: The Hemphill Folk Art Collection* (Washington: Smithsonian Institution Press, 1990). And see Herbert W. Hemphill, Jr. and Julia Weissman, *Twentieth Century American Folk Art and Artists* (New York: E.P. Dutton, 1974).

3 See E. Sutherland, *The Diaries of John Gregory Bourke* (Ann Arbor, MI: University Microfilm International, 1964), 309, which refers to "dolls of adobe and mud baked in the sun" as early as 1881. These figurines were made as toys for children. Sometimes, they were even made by the children themselves as toys. See Gary Witherspoon, "Navajo Social Organization". In *Southwest*, Vol 10 of *Handbook of North American Indians*, ed. by Alfonso Ortiz (Washington, D.C.: Smithsonian Institution, 1983), 529. The early mud toys have been noted to resemble fetishes found at Southwestern archaeological sites. Accordingly, the "mud toy" tradition may have existed for some time before it was referenced by John Gregory Bourke in 1881.

4 While various dates have been given for Willeto's birth, February 20, 1906 is the date shown on the family's tribal enrollment card. His death certificate, however, gives his date of birth as 1897. Also, while the census card spells his first name, "Charley," his death certificate spells it "Charlie." In early shows, the artist was sometimes incorrectly exhibited as "Alfred Walleto."

5 Robin sometimes signs his last name as "Wellito."

THE CENTRAL REGION

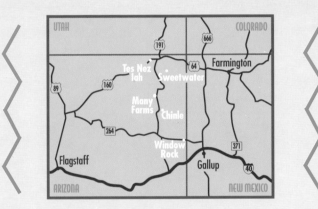

About twenty miles west of Farmington, Shiprock (elevation 7,178 feet) stands out above the grassy plain like the giant red sail of a schooner. The town of Shiprock, a short distance to the east of the pinnacle, is our entry point to the central region. Shiprock, New Mexico is located at the junction of U.S. 666, which winds up from Gallup, New Mexico, and U.S. 64, out of Farmington. Gallup, on the south, and Shiprock, on the north, anchor the eastern corners of our central region, which lies primarily in Arizona. As you journey through the Navajo Nation, you will want to visit several historic trading posts.

Foutz's Trading Company in Shiprock is a good place to start, not only because it looks pretty much as it did almost a hundred years ago, but also because it is well stocked with contemporary folk art. It is a yellow-stuccoed, modified pueblo-style building, with a parking lot facing U.S. 64. Bill and Kay Foutz, the present owners, are a friendly couple willing to chat at length with Native Americans and tourists alike, so take your time examining the merchandise. The building has served as a trading post since it was opened for business by Bruce Bernard in the early 1900s. It was remodeled by the Foutzes in 1982 when they took over the lease. Foutz's Trading Company still operates today very much as the business was conducted in earlier years—except that "pawn" has not been taken in since the mid-1970s when the U. S. Government passed strict regulations that, according to Bill Foutz, "required so much paperwork compliance that it made 'pawn' unprofitable on the reservation."

Bill Foutz is a descendant of a long line of Mormon traders. The patriarchal founder of the Foutz family empire was Joseph Lehi Foutz, who opened his first post in Tuba City in the 1890s. "At one time," says Bill Foutz, "the family operated as many as fifty stores in the region. We wholesaled to each other by wagon train. I still operate three posts myself, including the arts and crafts store at Teec Nos Pos."

Opposite: Woody Herbert, *White Brahma Bull*, c. 1987. Mixed media (carved wood, hair, dleesh, horns, and rope), 31" x 32" x 9".

Foutz specializes in and wholesales rugs. Two important weavers he handles are Matilda Damon and Florence Riggs, who has woven a portrait of Bill Foutz. Foutz takes credit for being the largest current dealer in Navajo rugs. "Quantity is way up," he explains. "Right now, I am buying four to five thousand rugs a year, but quality is getting harder to find, and very few really original pictorials ever come on the market." The trading company also carries Navajo pottery by Lorraine Williams and Alice Cling (among others) and folk art by Sandy and Bob Beyale and the Grawlers.

Because of his need to sell in volume, Bill Foutz sometimes practices the doctrine of "easy marketability." To get the rugs he wants to buy, we have heard him instruct artists as follows: "I don't want brown and yellow together. I don't like yellow, period! . . . I don't need Monument Valley scenes—bring me Yeibichai rugs." Fortunately, for those of us who love folk art, a few artists will defy their source of income and make art based on a personal vision rather than a trader's needs or preferences. (Note Florence Riggs' rug on page 143. Yellow and brown are present in the same rug; and sure enough, Foutz wouldn't buy that one.)

Fill up on gas before driving west past Shiprock Pinnacle itself (a towering mass that the Navajo call *Tsé Bit' q'í*, "rock with wings," or "winged rock"). If you are lucky, you will catch the rock at first light or sunset, and at roadside there will be a Navajo woman with her sheepdogs,

carrying a parasol against the heat of the sun, dressed in her long velvet finery, shepherding—tending to her flock of sheep and goats. You are now on the long stretch of road going toward Red Mesa and Sweetwater—time to reflect upon the art that you have seen, the people you have met, and the adventure ahead.

This beautiful land (the Dinétah) is about all that survives of the real West—the spiritual resting place of our pioneer forefathers. It was their "frontier philosophy," and their will-ingness to risk life and fortune in exchange for freedom, that brought most of them to America. Great risk is also an everyday occurrence for some of the Navajo artists of this area. Tom Yazzie and Ida Sahmie, for example, risked their eyesight breaking taboos involving their art. To do something that has never been done, to bare your soul to neighbor and stranger, this is a necessary ingredient of art. That is why their work reflects the values and spirit of all of us.

This handmade sign adorns New Post, one of the two buildings that comprise downtown Sweetwater.

The Dinétah, homeland of the Navajo, is a land of great rugged beauty. Everyone who learns about this area wants to take a pilgrimage with the family to Grand Canyon, Lake Powell, Monument Valley, and Canyon de Chelly (pronounced "d'Shay"). Tourists from all over the world visit these national landmarks, and the accommodations improve year after year.

But artists don't live in national parks. To find the artists, we had to travel thousands of miles of dirt roads and sometimes worse—unmarked dirt tracks.

The beauty of the off-road western frontier is hard to describe. Yes, there really are tall, snow-capped mountains and geological formations of red rock standing guard over sheep-nibbled plains. (Shiprock is one that is well known, but there are also Rough Rock, Black Rock, Round Rock, and on and on.) There are also fast-running washes and high mesas that catch the purple of sunset. Once off-road, however, there are no fast-food restaurants or tourist shops. It's a lonely place for the timid, without shade in summer and deeply rutted when there is snow or rain. There are no road signs, street addresses, or reliable maps. We have visited artists in places where no Anglo has gone before. Directions are given in terms of washes to cross, fences to open, and sheep camps to go around. And when the hogan of an artist is discovered, he or she may not be home, and there is no telephone so a future appointment can be arranged.

The post at Red Mesa is a last-chance supply stop if you're planning a dirt-track safari to Sweetwater. The home-cooked fried chicken is especially good for a take-along picnic. Since the Red Mesa post caters to the needs of the Navajo, it carries very little work of the Sweetwater artists nearby—just some jewelry and a few local rugs.

Finding Sweetwater is a real challenge. A mile east of the Red Mesa Trading Post on U.S. 160, there's a standard blue road marker pointing south, reading "Sweetwater 14 Miles." Tommy James, the trader at Red Mesa, advised us, tongue in cheek, "Sweetwater? I've never been there and don't know any white man who has. You go in there, you might not find your way out."

James's admonition didn't deter us. We were intent on finding Sweetwater because it is home to many fine Navajo folk artists: Elsie Benally, the Grawlers, Wilford and Lulu Yazzie, Dan Hot, Woody Herbert, Edith Herbert John, and Ron Malone. Hence, we refer to it as the "Folk Art Capital of Arizona."

However, there is no marked road to Sweetwater, and the Arizona road map calls the town by its Navajo name, *Totacon* (which is *Tó Łikan* in Young and Morgan's Navajo dictionary). So we were confused from the start by an unmapped land of sand and wind-blown tumbleweeds, dominated by towering Red Mesa and the distant peaks of the Carrizo Mountains, which shimmer blue in a sun-dried haze. We were on dirt tracks, criss-crossing similar tracks in and out of washes and up and down steep hills. The Navajo living in the area are clustered in distant camps, consisting of corrals for their livestock, hogans, and brush arbors. (These open-sided structures are generally constructed out of cedar poles. Their roofs are thatched with brush, generally oak branches because they maintain their dried leaves for several seasons before falling off. This brush covering provides protection from the sun, and the open sides allow breezes to penetrate. The arbors are used for meals in summer and often for sleeping in hot weather.)

Twenty-five miles south of U.S. 160, on the Navajo reservation in Arizona, we escaped from mud up to our door handles and tailgated under a sheltering cottonwood. A curious Navajo on horseback came by to see what was going on. He knew where Sweetwater was and pointed straight up the nob of a piñon-studded hill where no track was visible. Remembering the trader's warning, our first attempt at finding Sweetwater was over.

On our second try, a meter reader for the Navajo Electric Company passed us in a pick-up truck. He gave us directions: "Keep going right. You can't miss the town." But we did. Neither the highway sign nor the map indicated as much, but you can't get into Sweetwater in inclement weather; consequently, rain spoiled our third attempt—snow the fourth.

Then, in the spring of 1991, we met the potter Lorraine Williams, who had married into the most famous family of Navajo potters (that headed by Rose Williams). Lorraine Williams lives in a trailer park in Cortez, Colorado, but she was born a Sweetwater Yazzie. "I usually do my firing in a pit behind my hogan in Sweetwater," she said. "It's better there, somehow." With Williams's help, we finally reached the remote community on our fifth attempt.

The six to seven hundred Navajos here rely on their livestock to make a living. There are very few luxuries; some residents have electricity, making television possible; some have running water, but most bring in potable water by the barrel. Cooking is done over wood fires kept smoldering indoors in winter and outdoors in summer brush arbors, and there are no telephones, not even at the trading post, though a few staples like coffee, sugar, soup, and canned stew can be purchased there. School buses do journey into the community to take the children to schools in Red Mesa (grade school and high school), and the children are learning English, but Navajo tradition is still the core of their lives.

Above: Rose Williams's influence can be seen in the work of many famous Navajo potters. Opposite: Wilford Yazzie, *Female Yei Dancer*, 1987. Mixed media (carved and painted wood with yarn and chicken feathers), 15" x 6" x 3".

The children of Sweetwater enjoy a simple and safe existence. Most have horses and enjoy wonderful miles of open space—their playgrounds. For example, the children of Ray and Karen Growler, Desmond and Pamela, bragged about the goats they were raising at their grandfather's. Area unemployment is high, however, and young adults have a difficult time finding jobs, particularly during the recent recession. Young women learn to weave, and if they want to fill their hours in pursuit of this craft, they can always find a market for their work. However, figured by the hour, weavers' wages are very low. Many, like the Grawlers, move to nearby towns like Shiprock to obtain employment.

Johnnie Sammora, the young Navajo who purchased downtown Sweetwater in December 1991, operates from a long, brown, quonset-type building with a gas pump out front. There's a dilapidated stone structure nearby, built into a sandstone shelf, which also came with the deal. These establishments are affectionately called New Post and Old Post by the Navajo. And that's all there is in downtown Sweetwater.

There's an optimistic sign, "Open," in the front window of New Post, and the proprietor patiently sits behind the front counter, dreamily gazing at his packed mud parking lot, waiting for the occasional customer who needs to buy a few dollars' worth of gas to travel the red sand road to Rock Point in the west or to Red Mesa in the east.

Johnnie Sammora had never visited the folk artists, but several come into New Post. Thus, he was well aware that Sweetwater was gaining a reputation as an art center. "I plan to stock up on folk art," he assured us, "and maybe my post will prosper."

In the hollers of Kentucky, in the hills of West Virginia, in the delta of the Mississippi River, there are a number of self-taught artists, but nowhere in America have we discovered such a high per-capita concentration of serious talent. If these Navajo artists were working anywhere else, there would be tourist buses parked at their front doors.

From Sweetwater, you can retrace your steps to Red Mesa, but we prefer the unmarked

Above: The view from Ronald Malone's yard is, perhaps, an inspiration for his art. Opposite: Ronald Malone, *Cars and Trucks,* 1988-90. Carved sandstone and poster paint, approximately 2 1/4" x 4" x 2" each.

rock and sand track that leads west to Rock Point. The Point, rounded sandstone that rises like a gigantic arrowhead about fifty feet above the road, casts a sheltering shadow—making it a good place for a picnic. Once on U.S. 191 at Rock Point, you can take the road south to Many Farms or Chinle, where the natural wonders and historic Anasazi ruins of Canyon De Chelly can be enjoyed, or north towards Four Corners and *Tes Nez Iah* ("Tree Falling Across Wash and Making Bridge"), where there are folk artists waiting to be discovered.

The place called Four Corners, where the boundaries of Arizona, New Mexico, Utah, and Colorado meet, is a flat parking lot, surrounded by makeshift wooden booths protected from the sun by flapping torn canvas or shade poles. The buildings are fairly similar to the summer hogans of the Navajo.[1] Here, Indians hawk cheap rugs, baskets, and jewelry to tourists.

South and west of this well-known stop on U.S. Route 160, tourists usually bypass the long, low-slung grouping of buildings that constitute the trading post at Tes Nez Iah, Arizona. This is high country, surrounded by outcroppings of mesas, outlined in purple at sunset, slowly eroding down to sandstone bedrock.

Morris and Ann Butts, the traders at Tes Nez Iah, are connected to the rest of Arizona only by radio telephone, a welcome isolation. The Hathale family trades at the post. In fact, when we introduced ourselves, Morris Butts said that Roger Hathale had been in twice the previous day, but he could not tell us where Roger, a well-known medicine man, lived. "Somewhere out that way," he said, gesticulating toward a three-hundred square-mile area to the northwest.

Elsie Benally, *Rooster Rider*, 1986. Mixed media (sun-dried clay, paint, feathers, and turquoise eyes), 5 ¹/₂" x 5" x 2".

But Jan found us a guide—Lucille Johnson, a Navajo grade school teacher from Dennehotso, Arizona. Johnson willingly turned the family's laundry chores at the post over to her mother. "I know Roger Hathale," she explained. "He is an important medicine man, and his hogan is near our sheep camp."

Once off U.S. 160, we were on five miles of dirt track, punctuated by sharp, red rock in the places sand had drifted off the trail. Shortly after the turn onto dirt, there was a half fallen-over road sign—"Indian Route 6440," but the track was otherwise ungraded, unmapped, and unmarked. Johnson was looking for a windmill, and we found it, rusting in the wind. Later, Roger Hathale told us that it has been "busted—machinery no damn good—for a long time." The residents of the area had to carry their water in from the post at Tes Nez Iah.

At the windmill, we turned off Route 6440 on a journey that took the car almost straight up to the top of a mesa. For several miles, we twisted upward over yellow sandstone veined with green. The only road markings were the black tire stains left by pickup trucks. But Johnson kept saying, "Left here, right there," and soon we were on top of the world. We were told that we were the first Anglos to visit the Hathale family compound.

After leaving Tes Nez Iah, you will find Chinle, Arizona, a good place to spend a comfortable night. It is the location of the Canyon de Chelly National Monument, famous for its Anasazi petroglyphs. Established in 1931, the National Monument contains well over seven hundred ruin sites and cliff dwellings in the three major canyons encompassed in the National Monument. Navajos have lived in the area since the early seventeenth century. And it was here, in 1864, that cavalry under Kit Carson destroyed cornfields and orchards, capturing Navajo prisoners for the "Long Walk" to Bosque Redondo. All of Canyon de Chelly is included in the Navajo Reservation under the Treaty of 1868. Numerous Navajos live within the monument today.

The famous Indian trader Juan Lorenzo Hubbell (1853–1930) began operating at Chinle as early as 1886, building a substantial post there around 1900. However, few tourists came to Chinle in those days because of the bad roads; Hubbell sold out in 1917. Another trader, Sam Day, also established a trading post at Chinle in the early 1900s. The historic Thunderbird Lodge, located on the site of a former trading post, today handles Navajo arts and crafts, including a substantial number of rugs, both traditional and pictorial. The lodge will also arrange tours and horseback rides in the canyon.

We like to make arrangements for a Navajo guide to take us on an early morning horseback ride through Canyon de Chelly. The steep rock walls contain petroglyphs and Anasazi ruins. These early Indian settlers mysteriously disappeared from the area by 1300. While the reason for their leaving is not definitely known, long periods of drought and famine are suspected. In any event, they left behind sophisticated cave dwellings, pottery, and petroglyphs. The Navajos do not consider themselves related to the Anasazi. However, the Navajo refer to them reverently and never disturb their ruins. Thus, the ruins in this beautiful canyon have been preserved and look about as they must have looked when the Anasazi disappeared from Canyon de Chelly.

There's water in this vast canyon, even in the heat of summer. And many Navajo return here year after year, with their flocks of sheep and goats, to live in summer hogans and camps. On small patches of fertile land around their camps, they still grow the staples that sustained the Anasazi—beans, corn, and squash. This ride deep into the sandy floor of Canyon de Chelly is one of our favorites.

If you leave Chinle by noon, there is still time to visit Rough Rock and to see the famous murals depicting the historic Navajo struggle, which were done by artist Andrew Tsihnahjinnie on the walls of the Rough Rock Demonstration School cafeteria.

Although there is a traditional trading post in this small settlement, Rough Rock is best known for the impact it has had on Navajo education. In 1966, a community-controlled school, the Rough Rock Demonstration School, opened under contract with the Bureau of Indian Affairs. Based on the principles of community action, bilingual education, and Navajo cultural studies, the demonstration school was so successful that it led to the establishment of a Navajo Community College at Tsaile, Arizona, a few years later. This was the first college in the country to be established and run by Native Americans.

Most people stop at the old Hubbell Trading Post in Ganado, which is nestled in a small valley along the southern banks of the Colorado Wash, thirty-five miles south of Chinle. The store was operated by Juan Lorenzo Hubbell for over fifty years, starting in the late 1870s. Not only did Hubbell influence the development of rug making (the famous "Ganado red")

Tom Yazzie, *Navajo Nativity Scene*, c. 1964. Carved and painted cottonwood, figures range in height from 2 1/2" to 10".

and silversmithing, but he also helped his customers in a variety of ways and started several Navajos in business. Throughout his career, J. L. Hubbell had a very good relationship with Navajo leaders. At various times, he and his two sons owned as many as twenty four trading posts and other business and ranch properties.

After Hubbell's death in 1930, the post at Ganado continued under the management of the Hubbell family until 1967, when it was purchased by the federal government as a National Historic Site. The Southwest Parks and Monuments Association operates the post as a living history exhibit. Merchandise—saddles and harnesses, and even a bird cage—still hangs from unpainted vigas, and it looks like the post Juan Lorenzo Hubbell left behind. Although a few supplies are still carried, the post's original function has ceased to exist. Tourists by the busloads come through here each day. You can somewhat escape from the tourists in a back room where Bill Malone, the post's present manager, presides over a counter, selling fine jewelry. On the room's unpainted wooden board floor, there are piles of rugs laid out for sale according to quality, type, and color. This room, with the old Hubbell collection of baskets nailed to walls and ceiling, as Juan Lorenzo preferred to display them, is a good place to shop, rest, and gossip with dealers, pickers, and collectors. The thick adobe walls of the post also preserve the morning's coolness, even in the heat of midday.

In Window Rock (*Tségháhoodzání*, "the rock with a hole in it"), underneath the giant eye with its opening forty-seven feet in diameter, are the simply constructed government buildings of the Navajo Nation.

In the early 1930s, when John Collier was Commissioner of Indian Affairs, he was shown the giant rock and immediately declared that it should be the center of administration for the Navajo Tribe. Following Collier's plans, stone was quarried, ponderosa pine felled, and a Council House built in the form of a great ceremonial hogan. The Atchison, Topeka and Santa Fe Railway Company gave the tribe a large bell to commemorate the service of the thousands of Navajo who have labored for the railroad; this symbolic bell is still used to call the seventy-four elected councilmen to session. The business of the Navajo Nation is conducted in English and Navajo, and an interpreter is present.

The Navajo government and the Bureau of Indian Affairs have outgrown their original stone quarters. Today, Window Rock and its sister city, Fort Defiance, have become the commercial centers of the Nation. The Navajo Nation Museum, displaying works by a number of artists in this book, as well as a large arts and craft center, run by the Navajo, are located at the main intersection. Next door, there is a modern hotel and restaurant. The area is the site of an annual tribal fair, held in the late summer, which attracts many tourists and people from all over the reservation. A new grandstand for observing rodeo events, horse racing, and the evening pageant and entertainment was constructed recently.

Window Rock and Fort Defiance are busy and growing towns. Nevertheless, be prepared to stop and give up your right-of-way to an occasional loose horse or a herd of cattle.

In addition to towns like Window Rock, Fort Defiance, Shiprock, and Chinle, our central region contains vast areas of almost unexplored land that can be reached only by dirt tracks. The Navajo here are dependent upon their livestock, and when the snows of winter cover the earth, subsistence for cattle and people must be air-dropped to remote hogans. But this is a beautiful land that has shaped the creative spirit of the Diné.

Elsie Benally

Elsie Benally, along with Mamie Deschillie (page 42), is credited for reviving the Navajo tradition of making mud toys. The work of both these artists is sculptural in form, designed as art rather than the children's playtoys of the earlier years. Benally began making them in the spring of 1983 and was the first to bring them to the attention of Indian trader Jack Beasley in Farmington. (Beasley had asked Benally and several other Navajo women, including Mamie Deschillie, if they could make something they remembered as children mud toys were the result.)

We have never been able to interview this artist even though we have driven the steep track up to her home on at least five occasions. She lives with her husband, Sam Benally, in a plywood and shingle bungalow about forty feet to the north of artist Dan Hot's house. Benally, we are told, is in her middle thirties or early forties and does not speak English. She is related to Dan Hot (probably a stepdaughter), and that is all we know.

How much of her work she does by herself is not certain. Dan Hot, who is known for his fabric-covered bulls, sometimes tells Jack Beasley that he was the first to make the mud toys and that he taught Elsie Benally her craft. It is likely that Sam Benally, Elsie Benally's husband, helps in some way. While Beasley usually deals with Sam Benally, he is uncertain as to the extent of the husband's participation in this art form. We do know that Sam Benally sometimes makes wagons out of wood; Elsie Benally will make the drivers out of clay, place a whole family of mud toys in the back, including a nursing mother and baby, or, perhaps, some farm animals—sheep or goats.

Opposite: Elsie Benally, *Women's Basketball Team*, 1991. Mixed media (sun-dried clay and paint with wool hair, mounted on cardboard), approximately 6" x 2" x 2" each.

But let the mud toys speak for themselves! They are highly creative and fragile sculptures ranging between two inches and four inches in height. The basic material is sun-fired mud (water and earth). They are decorated with all sorts of found objects—bits of cloth, fur, stone, paper, and sequins. Benally makes a great many sheep and goats covered with real wool, and her animals usually have black faces. She also makes cowboys and Indians mounted on horseback and groups of figures—uniformed basketball teams and tourists, cameras held at the ready—staring into space.

Curiously, the only easy way to tell Benally's figures from those of Mamie Deschillie is that Benally's usually have flat, noseless faces.

Elsie Benally has been exhibited at the Wheelwright Museum of the American Indian, and her work is included in its permanent collection. Benally's mud toys are extremely popular in the Southwest, and Indian trader Jack Beasley and other traders have sold hundreds of them through galleries and stores throughout the region.

Ray Growler

If you admire a flock of realistic-looking lambs, goats, or sheep with real hides, fur, and horns standing next to a kiva fireplace in Santa Fe, chances are the animals were made by Ray Growler.

Ray and his wife, Karen Growler, share a house in Shiprock with their four children, but the goats and sheep are made at the home of Ray Growler's parents, Jimmy and Irene Growler, in Sweetwater. Ray Growler was born here, on the rocky hillside where his folks still live, and attended nearby Red Mesa High School. Nowadays, he frequently makes the hour-long drive west from Shiprock to visit his family and work on his art.

Growler is also an experienced sheet metal worker who finds employment in Alamosa, Colorado, and other places in winter. "But I got my hand caught in some machinery," he says, "and I'd like to make art full-time. However, for right now, I do sheet metal in winter and folk art in summer."

Opposite: Ray Growler, *Billy Goats*, c. 1990. Mixed media (carved wood with horns, wool, and hide), 28" x 28" x 2" and 22" x 22" x 10".

He was not the first to make the figures. Johnson Antonio, with the help of his wife, Lorena, began making them in about 1984—sheep and goats, with carved and painted faces (most of the other carvers cover the animal's face with hide or wool), proudly bearing horns that the Antonios found in the fields surrounding their home in Lake Valley. "We made them first," Lorena Antonio declared, "but so many copied us that we quit two years later."

Ray Growler denies, however, that he copied Johnson Antonio. "I never saw one of his carvings," he states in defense of his work. "I was the first. I invented the sheep and goats. I was making a sawhorse, up at my dad's, and it looked like a sheep. Mom had a pelt hanging on a line to cure, so I glued it on the horse. It looked so good I took it to Beasley [Beasley-Manning Trading Post in Farmington, New Mexico]. Beasley said 'great!' and put me to work."

Growler uses cedar and roughs out his animals with a chain saw and an ax. He glues home-cured pelts to this rough frame. (The pelts are washed first, scraped clean of fat and gristle, and soaked in a commercial salt-tanning solution purchased in Gallup, New Mexico. Then, they are hung on an ordinary clothes line to dry and whiten in the sun.) The finished animal has the natural color of the wool—shades of white, gray, brown, and black. At first, Growler was able to acquire all the horns and pelts he needed from animals that had been slaughtered by neighbors for meat or had been killed by coyotes. "The Navajo people sell pelts to each other for five dollars each," he explains. "Lately, however, I've made so many animals that I've had to buy horns from the San Juan Slaughter House in Farmington. A pair of big billy goat or ram horns can cost me up to thirty-five dollars."

The artist takes pride in the fact that he does all of the work himself. "Karen helps brush out the wool," he says. "My father makes some buffalo covered with brown lamb's wool, and my sister, Ruby Growler, sometimes makes lambs and goats, but . they sell them under their own names."

Growler has a legitimate complaint over the attribution of his work to others: "Many galleries and shops put my name on animals which were made by other families because they can get more money for mine than theirs," he declares. Growler is right on this point. As often happens, when a Navajo is successful, others have joined in.

Ray Growler's delightful animals have become very popular and can be purchased at museum shops, galleries, and stores throughout the Southwest.

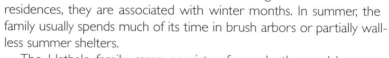

The Hathale Family

When we finally arrived at our destination, the Hathale family compound, the view was of a valley shimmering in haze. But the dominant feature, perched on the mesa's crest, is a traditional mud hogan with its door facing east toward the sunrise.

Relatively few contemporary Navajo still live in this type of dwelling made out of logs and bark and covered roughly with red mud. While the ancient or "forked stick" hogans were conical in shape (constructed of forked poles, covered with logs, brush, or mud), the hogans more often seen today are round, heptagonal, or octagonal structures, constructed of logs or stone when such materials are available, with a hard-packed dirt floor and a smoke hole in the center. To the extent hogans are still used as residences, they are associated with winter months. In summer, the family usually spends much of its time in brush arbors or partially wall-less summer shelters.

The Hathale family camp consists of corrals, the mud hogan, and two other dwellings of plywood. This is home to Roger, his wife Dinah, son Bruce, and his son's wife, Susie, and their two children.

Hataałii (which has been anglicized in this case to Hathale by all family members, despite the fact that Dennis Hathale's census card spells it the traditional way) means singer, the conductor of traditional Navajo blessing and curative ceremonies. Since the knowledge and correct performance of ritual can cure or prevent disease, bring danger under control, and restore harmony, the singer is an important member of the Navajo community.

Roger Hathale, known as "the medicine man from Tes Nez Iah," is the patriarch of a large family (he and Dinah had seven boys and six girls), but only two of his sons, Dennis and Bruce, are engaged in making sandpaintings on used bed sheets, called "muslins." Hathale is part of a long tradition: "father, grandfather, and I don't know how many others before me were medicine men," he proudly states.

Roger Hathale was born in 1918. He had four years of formal education in Shiprock and doesn't speak much English or give many interviews. But with the help of our guide for the day, Lucille Johnson, the reluctant old man talked about his religion and the origins of the now famous "muslins."

The Navajo Way, the ordained way of life on earth for the Navajo—harmony, balance, and order—has been taught and preserved largely through oral tradition and through pictographs, faithfully reproduced by generations of singers.

Opposite: Hathale Family (attributed to Roger Hathale), *Female Snake Person,* c. 1986. Mineral pigments on percale bedsheet (muslin), 10 1/4 x 9 3/4 .

When the medicine man, or singer, performs a ceremony, he makes sandpaintings on the dirt floor of the patient's hogan. The patient sits or lies upon them, and illness is left in the sand that is swept up in the morning and scattered. These fragile pictorials on packed mud explain Navajo legend and history and transmit the religion of the Diné to succeeding generations. "They must be made right to work." In fact, there really is no word for art in Navajo—"to be made right" is about as close as you can come.

The medicine man may keep a diary called "memory aids" containing sketches of successful sandpaintings. Historically, some of these early records were on muslin, and examples can be found. Roger Hathale told us that he did not have memory aids, but his sons said that they relied upon them. We believe that he just didn't want us to see his sacred ceremonial material.

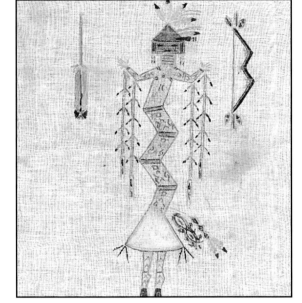

The Hathale muslins were discovered in the early 1980s by Jack Beasley. Beasley said that Roger Hathale had been regularly pawning old Navajo necklaces, bracelets, and concho belts for some time, and then one day, "he brought in a muslin, and I asked him for more." Hathale told Beasley that this first muslin was made by his son Bruce. However, because the father brought it into his store, Beasley believes Roger Hathale made it.

Roger Hathale explained the creation of his art form as follows: "I was looking around for something my boys could do and felt that they could reproduce the sandpaintings I made for ceremonies, as long as they were accurate. If others did this type of art they would be harmed, but I have the power to protect my boys. The idea was mine, but I have never made one myself. Certain figures would bring harm, but I will not let these be sold." The muslins are not made for, or used, in ceremonies—they are true folk art.

As our 4x4 vehicle was about to slide over the edge of the mesa and begin its slippery sandstone decent, Lucille Johnson pointed out a circle made of logs and a rack holding ridge poles. "This is where a tepee is erected and Roger Hathale conducts Native American Church ceremonies," she said. "My mother and grandmother do not approve of this church and its use of peyote, but many Navajo have joined." The

Church is a religious movement that spread to the Navajo between 1930 and 1950 and has grown steadily since that time. Its ritual involves eating the peyote cactus (*Lophophora williamsii*), a substance containing various alkaloids, the best known of which is mescaline. While the effect is one of mild hallucination, evidence to date does not support allegations concerning the negative effects of peyote (taken in moderation during church gatherings). With the spread of the Native American Church among the Navajos, there was fear that the traditional ceremonial system might decline. This did not happen. Members of the Church remained active in traditional ceremonies, and many medicine men, like Roger Hathale, also became "Roadmen," those who conduct Native American Church ceremonies. The art of the Hathales, however, is derived from Navajo traditions, unrelated to the Native American Church.

Bruce Hathale, born in 1956, was raised on top of the mesa in Tes Nez Iah. He completed about eleven years of boarding school in Blanding, Utah. Bruce Hathale, his wife, Susie George, and their two children live in the family compound overlooking the post at Tes Nez Iah.

There is virtually no employment in this sparsely populated area, which is completely isolated from the rest of Arizona in winter storms or heavy rainfall. Most of the Navajo rely on their herds of sheep and goats, and some of the women weave.

"In 1983," Bruce relates, "my father had the idea for me to do sandpaintings on old

bed sheets. I did it first and then my brother Dennis joined in. I work from a book I bought and from my father's drawings [memory aids]. Sometimes Roger won't let me copy one because of tradition, but sometimes he says, 'go ahead.'" Bruce Hathale has to "bum" his rides into Farmington. "I don't own a truck," he admits, "but I try to bring Jack Beasley at least one muslin every Tuesday, and Susie helps with the painting."

It's sometimes hard to distinguish between the brothers' work. Bruce makes fewer drawings than Dennis, but generally his have finer lines and more detail, though the colors may be less vibrant and the figures not as bold. The earlier brownish muslins with the ragged edges are considered the most valuable. As the brothers made more muslins, the work took on a cleaner look, and the colors became brighter.

On the day we visited the Hathales, Bruce Hathale showed us a muslin depicting a legendary spirit, Monster Slayer, and Lucille Johnson commented as follows: "I have seen many sandpaintings on board. They are sold to tourists in stores, but those sand boards are more like designs—not really right. Bruce's Monster Slayer is the real thing. I didn't know a Navajo could do that."

Dennis Hathale was born in 1961 and attended boarding school in Blanding, Utah, for about ten years. He considers himself an apprentice medicine man. He prays that, "someday—sometime, I will carry on after my father, but since 1986, I have been making muslins." Dennis and Lynda also attend the Native American Church, in addition to traditional Navajo ceremonies like the Blessingway, which his father performed to protect them against harm. "When our son turned eleven," Lynda says, "we took him to his first Native American Church service. He seemed to enjoy the ceremony."

Dennis and Lynda Hathale are more urbanized than the other members of the family. They live in a small, tucked-out-of-sight frame house in Farmington, New Mexico, where Dennis is employed on temporary jobs for construction companies.

From Dennis and Lynda, we were were able to obtain some additional information about the muslin-making process. The basic material is used bedsheets purchased from the Salvation Army, flea fairs, and the like. Lynda Hathale points out that "the more cotton in the sheeting, the better, because cotton absorbs our sand mixture. Unfortunately, we have bought so many that good sheets are now hard to find."

Hathale Family (attributed to Bruce Hathale), *Big Thunder with Four Thunderbirds,* c. 1987. Mineral pigments on percale bedsheet (muslin), 43" x 32".

The sheets are cut to size and rolled in a home-invented gesso mixture of earth and water. After a thorough soaking in this mixture, the sheets are hung on a line to dry, and the excess mud is scraped off.

"Colored sand and mineral pigments," according to Dennis, "are the only source for the paint used by Roger in [ceremonial] sandpainting. The medicine men know where to find it and buy and trade the colors among themselves. All we do is mix them with water and paint it on."

Dennis further informs us that "the drawings must be right. I can't mess 'em up, and they must be approved by Roger or they will bring us bad luck." Whereupon Lynda volunteers the following: "I help with the muslins, but if I were to make one while pregnant, that would be taboo." As with pottery and basket making, many Navajos consider various taboos or ritual restrictions applicable to this type of work. The Hathales believe that if Lynda were to work while pregnant and the drawing was not exactly right, the baby might be born deformed. Thus, it is safer to defer work on the art during the period of pregnancy.

Opposite: Hathale Family (attributed to Dennis Hathale), *Endless Snake*, c. 1987. Mineral pigments on percale bedsheet (muslin), 21" x 21".

During the last year or so, the gesso forming the background color of the work has taken on a rose/pink color, the color of sandstone prevalent throughout Arizona and New Mexico. Beasley is partly responsible for this new look. "The first collectors," he says, "like you, were looking for authentic primitive work, but the market soon grew more diversified. Collectors wanted more decorative muslins without ragged edges, and they didn't like to see sand smudge off their purchases. So I suggested that the Hathales add Elmer's Glue to their mixtures to make the paintings more permanent and mentioned that earth colors might be more pleasing as backgrounds than their original dull mixture."

Clearly, today, as in the past, traders can have an impact on the direction taken by artists who, in many instances, rely on the trader for access to markets. On the other hand, most of the folk artists we have met now have access to transportation, which means that they can drive to more distant cities if the traders become too interfering. Accordingly, the artists are in many respects more independent—freer to pursue their own vision than at any time in the past.

Woody Herbert

Woody Herbert is a pioneer folk artist from Sweetwater. He is known for his silvery gray and white-humped Brahma bulls, made from cottonwood and decorated with sheep wool and real horns.

We have interviewed two of Herbert's daughters who are artists (Lulu Herbert Yazzie and Edith Herbert John), but Woody Herbert has eluded us. He is married to Anne Herbert and lives in a family compound, which includes the home of his son-in-law and daughter, Wilford and Lulu Herbert Yazzie, on a mesa high above the trading post at Sweetwater. The view from his ceremonial hogan over the valley toward the Carrizo Mountains is nothing short of spectacular. We are told that Herbert was born in 1926 or 1927, that he did not attend school, and that he does not speak English. He maintains a herd of sheep and goats that produce the only cash crop of this extended family.

In his younger days, Herbert was a bronco buster extraordinaire. Herds of wild horses roam the Sweetwater plains, where there are no fences. Herbert used to corral them, break them, and sell them. But he can no longer work in this capacity; Woody Herbert has a heart problem that has also made him cut back on roughing out the cottonwood he uses to create art objects with a hatchet.

Herbert was one of the first artists in Sweetwater to begin making contemporary folk art, and he has undoubtedly influenced others, including members of his family. The first

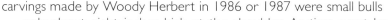

{ Right: Woody Herbert, *Brahma Bull*, c. 1986. Mixed media (carved wood with hair, dleesh, paint, and horns), 35" x 44" x 16".

carvings made by Woody Herbert in 1986 or 1987 were small bulls only about eight inches high at the shoulder. As time went by, the animals became larger; presently, they range upwards to about thirty-eight inches and stand on spindle-legged boards. The larger the Brahma bulls became, the stronger the presence.

The animals are painted with ordinary house paint, but some of the whites in the early work are dleesh, a white clay used by the Navajo to paint their bodies for ceremonies. Dleesh is water soluble and fragile. The bulls proudly bear real goat horns, and goat or sheep wool is used in the genital areas.

Woody Herbert has made other animals—horses, crows, and the ever-popular coyote. However, he is not as prolific as some of the other carvers, and his reputation rests on his famous silver and white Brahma bulls. Herbert's animals have found their way into the Wheelwright Museum of the American Indian and are included in many important private collections.

{ Woody Herbert, *White-Faced Bull*, c. 1986. Mixed media (painted wood with horns, thumbtacks, wool, and string), 8" x 11" x 7 1/2".

Dan Hot

Dan Hot doesn't speak more than a dozen words of English, but one of his fabric-covered bulls was featured in a color photograph in the St. Louis Post-Dispatch on September 21, 1987, and another grazes in the executive offices of the Museum of American Folk Art in New York City.

Dan Hot, born in 1932, is a resident of Sweetwater. That's where we caught up with him recently, tending a cooking fire in the family brush arbor. We had been dallying around the area for the whole morning, trying to find and photograph Hot, because Johnnie Sammora at New Post had informed us: "He'll be back. Just bought some gas to go to Rock Point to visit a medicine man."

Photographing Hot wasn't easy: there were no younger family members about to translate; he was wearing a black hat, standing in a sun-dappled, smoky arbor; and he held up one finger—just one exposure allowed.

Occasionally, the artist has been exhibited as "Hat" because of a trader's mistake in reading Hot's signature in a pawn ledger book. The confusion was subsequently cleared up, however, and the work is now generally attributed correctly to "Dan Hot."

Dan Hot is a relative of Elsie Benally, who lives nearby. He is best known for his imaginative, colorful, crudely carved-out bulls, standing no more then two feet at the shoulders (he occasionally fashions other animals such as buffaloes). Because of the way the animals are dressed—in discarded cloth, furniture fabric, and even secondhand ultrasuede—the creatures amuse and delight their audience. The color of their hides depends entirely on the material available at local flea markets, but Hot adds realism to the animals by nailing goat horns or carved wooden horns onto their frames, sometimes emphasizing their rather specific exaggerated genitalia. Dan Hot's vision is unique in the history of Navajo art, and the growing reputation of this artist is well deserved.

Opposite: Dan Hot, *Red Bull and White Bull,* c. 1986 (red bull) and c. 1991 (white bull). Mixed media (wood covered with ultrasuede, goat horns, and paint), red bull measures 17 1/2" x 26 1/2" x 8", white bull measures 13" x 17 1/2" x 6 1/2".

Dan Hot, *Striped Bull and Buffalo,* c. 1987. Mixed media (wood, furniture fabric, and paint), striped bull measures 12 1/2" x 19" x 5 1/2", buffalo measures 12" x 20 1/2" x 4".

Edith Herbert John

Lorena Herbert, one of Woody Herbert's seven children, took time off from her family babysitting chores to guide us to the home of her married sister, Edith Herbert John, on a high mesa above the canyon in which Sweetwater is nestled. Edith was delighted with the surprise visit. Even though only eight miles separate the sisters, communication is difficult without telephones, and social calls are a rarity.

Both girls attended Sweetwater's isolated Plymouth Brethren's Immanual Mission School (founded in 1924) through the eighth grade. Because of their schooling, the two sisters are fairly fluent in English as well as Navajo.

Opposite: Edith Herbert John, *Two Owls*, c. 1990. Carved and painted wood, 11 1/2" x 7" x 9" each.

Edith John's husband, Guy, is employed at the Red Mesa High School. They live with their two children in a silver-bullet house trailer. Unlike many others in the Sweetwater community, including those at her father's family compound, the Johns are connected to electricity and have a large TV dish.

Edith John, the newest member of Woody Herbert's family to become an artist, has been an overnight success. She started carving cottonwood in 1990 "for fun, working with Dad making toys for the children, but now," she frankly admits, "I do it because I need the money." Her style, however, is clearly her own and is not influenced by the work of her famous father.

To date, John has made a series of stylized owl critters. She is a colorist—the owls come in just about every imaginable color, but they usually have yellow beaks, yellow legs, and round, black eyes surrounded by yellow circular lids, which set-off their flat, saucy faces from the rest of their bodies.

Owls are taboo. Their presence can bring bad luck to a home. But John rationalizes her preoccupation with owls as follows: "My neighbors don't know I'm making owls. They can't fear for me, and they [the carvings] bring me only good luck—MONEY!"

Ronald Malone

The land in front of Ronald Malone's home above Sweetwater falls off sharply toward the Carrizo Mountains to the east. It's a view to kill for! But just below the prow of his hill, Malone has anchored six junked cars in a neat row (see page 72). They are a symbol of Navajo dependence on transportation and, perhaps, a source of inspiration for his sandstone carvings.

Ronald Malone was born in 1946, near Gallup, New Mexico, and "didn't bother much with school. But I always loved cars and trucks," he remembers. "Model T's and Jeeps. I used to sit and watch them go by and make wooden ones to play with, when I should have been in school."

Below: Ronald Malone, *Green Sedan,* 1990. Carved sandstone and poster paint, 5" x 10 ½" x 4".

Malone discovered his latent talent in art during the early 1980s. "Everybody [in Sweetwater] was making everything," he said. "So I thought I'd make something different. I cut a truck playtoy out of sandstone, painted it black (because that was the only color I had), and took it to Jack Beasley in Farmington. He bought it right then."

That black Model T was the first of the several hundred cars and trucks Malone has made. Nowadays, they are brightly painted in many colors with poster paints—delivery trucks, antique models, and up-to-date, stylized versions of everything that's on the road.

Malone rough-cuts his vehicles out of sandstone, readily available in the washes behind his home, with an ordinary hand-held carpenter's saw. Sandpaper would not stand up to the task of smoothing the stone, so Malone has devised a novel

method for polishing: he vigorously rubs the partially completed carving on the rough surfaces of an ordinary concrete block until the stone has the patina of fired clay. The finishing details—wheels, fenders, doors—are sculpted with the aid of files. "Files don't hold up to the stone," the artist asserts. "I have to keep buying new ones at flea markets."

Sometimes, Malone glues teardrop headlights onto his model vehicles, and he occasionally identifies his delivery trucks with labels like "Chesse & Milk." Usually, however, they are recognizable models that need no labels. Malone's cars and trucks are not to scale but appear as romantic versions of the original—sometimes elongated and sometimes foreshortened—depending upon the artist's vision and imagination. He breathes life into them and does not simply sit back and rely on designs originating in Detroit or Tokyo.

The Malones have three boys and three girls, "but my cars and trucks," the artist says, "are not for them to play with—they're for sale. I don't raise sheep and goats like my neighbors. I rely on the money my carvings bring."

Malone has been exhibited at the Wheelwright Museum of the American Indian in Santa Fe and the Museum of Northern Arizona in Flagstaff.

Ronald Malone, *Delivery Truck: Chesse and Milk,* 1991. Carved sandstone and poster paint, 3 1/4" x 7" x 2 3/4".

Andrew Tsihnahjinnie

The legendary artist Andrew Tsihnahjinnie[2] maintains a family home near Rough Rock (*Tséch'izhi*), Arizona. Tsihnahjinnie has given the date of his birth as 1908, 1909, and 1916. He prefers the later date at the moment, perhaps because it takes away some years. To add to the confusion, the day of his birth is variously given as February 14 or November 14.[3] His Army discharge shows Tsihnahjinnie's birth date as November 14, 1916. The place of his birth, however, is not in dispute—a hogan at Owl Springs, perched high on a cliff overlooking Tsihnahjinnie's Rough Rock home.

Opposite: Andrew Tsihnahjinnie, *The Buffalo Hunt*, c. 1990. Mixed media (Bondo over coat-wire armature, paint, rabbit fur, feathers, and leather), horse and rider measure 16 1/4" x 16 1/2" x 11", buffalo measures 8 1/2" x 10 1/2" x 5".

Tsosie Tsihnahjinnie, the artist's son, read to us the following description of his father's account of his early schooling. They are notes he has taken with the intent of someday writing a biography of his famous parent: "In those days, it was the practice to round up Navajo boys in the fall of every year and take them off to boarding school. I was taken to several schools—first at Chinle, then Holbrook, and later Fort Apache. I would return home to Rough Rock at the first opportunity. At Fort Apache, for instance, seven of us boys 'borrowed' Apache horses and rode off for home. I returned home safely, but a few days later a policeman came for me on horseback, handcuffed me, and took me back." Despite Tsihnahjinnie's constant truancy, he graduated from eighth grade at Fort Apache in 1932 and made the long trip (wagon and bus to Gallup and train to Santa Fe) to enroll in the Santa Fe Indian School. There, he made some drawings on board in manual training which brought him to the attention of Dorothy Dunn; he became a member of her famous studio. (Tsihnahjinnie's earliest work is signed in the lower right-hand corner with a small delicate drawing of a hogan, loom, and sheep corral, illustrating the creed of the Navajo—the Navajo way of life, which is his.)

Dorothy Dunn taught at the Santa Domingo Pueblo Day School in 1928 and then obtained a degree from the Art Institute of Chicago in 1932. Upon her return to New Mexico, she began teaching fifth grade at the Santa Fe Indian School and opened an art studio in the school's craft room.

Dunn encouraged "creative spirit" among Indians, but she also dictated that the subject matter be Native American and insisted that her pupils paint in a uniform, flat, realistic style she believed to be Indian, which undoubtedly discouraged some individuality. The resulting work is beautiful, of high quality, and records with great accuracy

American Indian life of the time. The Dunn Studio drawings are of enormous historical value, and many, including ten by Tsihnahjinnie, are now part of the permanent collection of the Museum of Indian Arts and Culture in Santa Fe. (Dorothy Dunn remained with the studio until 1938, leaving its care with her assistant after that date. The studio continued until 1962, when it became part of the Institute of American Indian Arts.)

Andrew Tsihnahjinnie remembers that he paid his way to the Chicago World's Fair in 1933 by selling his drawings, and that, while attending the fair, he a had a job translating Navajo for a medicine man. Tsihnahjinnie graduated from the Santa Fe Indian School in 1936. He joined the U.S. Army Air Force (1941–1945) and served in the Pacific. Tsihnahjinnie recalls that while in the Air Force, he painted "Dirty Girty" on the noses of P-38 fighter planes.

In 1954, the artist married Minnie June Lee McGirt, who is half-Seminole and half-Creek. Minnie Tsihnahjinnie worked at the Rough Rock School, as a home economics teacher, until her retirement in 1992. The couple had four boys and three girls. An amusing family story is told about the origin of the present complicated spelling of their last name: the artist spelled his name Tsinajinnie at the time of the marriage. But shortly afterwards, while purchasing a house in Phoenix, Minnie spelled her husband's name phonetically "Tsihnah-jin-nie," and that spelling is used today.

Opposite: Andrew Tsihnahjinnie, *Men and Women at River*, c. 1930s. Watercolor on paper, 14 1/4" x 21".

Tsihnahjinnie became an illustrator of books. The early works (for instance, *Peetie the Pack Rat* and *Silver Magic*) were children's books that are collector's items today. Published in Window Rock during the 1930s, they were at least partially funded with government money. Probably the artist's most important contribution was the heroic illustrations for *Navajo History*, which was published by the Rough Rock Press (no longer active) in 1971. This is one of the first illustrated compilations of the tribe's prehistory; it is used extensively in curriculums aimed at teaching Navajo children their own history and legends.

Tsihnahjinnie also completed a series of large murals, in the same flat style as his illustrations, on the walls of the Rough Rock School. These murals are historically important because they depict the religion, history, and struggle of the Navajo people.

Our favorite works by this artist, however, are the occasional carvings or sculptures that he makes for his own enjoyment. These pieces, made from wood, stone, or even Bondo (a hard substance used to repair automobile dents), are completely different from the work depicting the heroic Navajo or the tight line drawings made in the Dunn Studio. They express the imaginative personal vision of their creator, and they are the reason for his inclusion in this volume.

Tsihnahjinnie has received many honors during his long life. In addition to his drawings in the permanent collection of the Museum of Indian Arts and Culture, he is represented in the collection of The Heard Museum in Phoenix and many other institutions and private collections. And, to sum up an illustrious career, Governor Fife Symington designated Tsihnahjinnie a living treasure of Arizona on September 17, 1991.

Lorraine Williams

"The potteries talk to you," Lorraine Williams reverently explains. "When I am feeling down, they say 'go rest, leave me alone.' When it's a good day they say, 'start working.'"

Williams, born in 1955, was raised in a hogan in Sweetwater, Arizona. She was originally given the name Tsi (daughter) by her medicine-man father, Donald Yazzie. "And," she says, "even though I was educated by the Mormons [ten grades at Intermountain Indian Boarding School in Brigham City, Utah], I am still a traditional Navajo. When one of my children is sick, for instance, I'd take the child first to a medicine man, and then, only if he advises, to a hospital."

Williams lives in a house trailer in Cortez, Colorado. Her husband, George, is a plant operator for Mobile Oil Company at Aneth, Utah; they have two girls and two boys. George Williams is one of Rose Williams' sons, brother of potters Alice Cling, Sue Ann Williams, and Susie Williams Crank. "I grew up in a family of potters," he relates. "Mother was always saying: 'Do pottery! You can buy a vehicle or school clothes.' But I never wanted to get my hands in it."

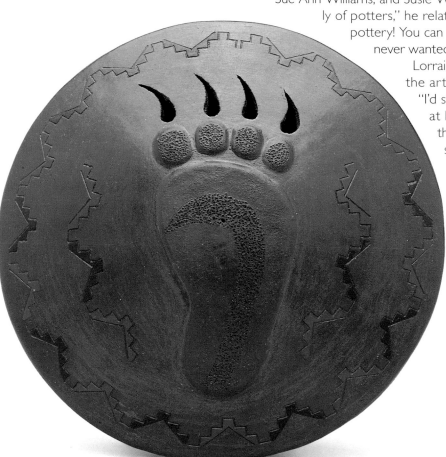

Lorraine Williams, however, did want to learn the art of pottery making. "At first," she says, "I'd stand around watching my mother-in-law at her Shonto Corner home—pretending that I wasn't. And then I'd go home and try. I stay home a lot with the kids, and so I like doing art from the trailer. In the beginning it was just for fun, but now it's my income."

"One winter," Williams remembers. "I got a job working for the Mesa Verde Pottery [a commercial operation located between Mesa

Lorraine Williams, *Bear Paw Pot*, 1992. Fired clay with piñon pitch and slip, 4 ¹/₂" height x 31" circumference.

Verde and Cortez, Colorado], painting Ute designs on machine-molded blanks. This wasn't for me, so I began making my own about five years ago."

Williams's pottery is made in the traditional Navajo manner. Her shapes and designs are delicate, graceful, and innovative, and she uses color sparingly—russets and yellows—by applying clay slips as highlights. In her early work, Williams etched recognizable Navajo symbols into the clay in place of the biyo'. Lately, her drawings have become more intricate—bears, Yei figures, and horned moons (pictured at right). According to Williams, "Horned moons appear in sandpainting when there is an eclipse of the sun. A baby born at this time is in danger of bad health, and blessings are required to prevent bad luck for all." Lorraine Williams has even made a few pieces that abandon the vessel shape entirely. These are hollow, cylindrical works that contain unusual design elements like a bear's claw breaking through the surface.

Until last year, the artist believed that it brought her good luck to make the fifty-mile trip home to her family hogan in Sweetwater to fire her pots in an open pit. Lately, however, she has been saving herself this trip—burning cedar bark in a neighbor's large fireplace instead.

Lorraine Williams has been featured at Packard's Indian Trading Company, the prestigious gallery on the Plaza in Santa Fe. Her work also appears frequently in galleries as distant as Los Angeles. Her first Indian Market appearance was in 1992; she went home with a second place ribbon, losing out by a narrow margin to her famous sister-in-law, Alice Cling.

Lorraine Williams, *Horned Moons,* c. 1991. Fired clay with piñon pitch, slip, and incised designs, 5 1/2" height x 17" circumference.

Wilford and Lulu Yazzie

Wilford and Lulu Herbert Yazzie (born 1946 and 1959, respectively) are two pioneer Sweetwater folk artists. "We weren't working or nothing," Wilford says. "The Nez family down in Chinle was making goats, my father-in-law [Woody Herbert] was making bulls—so I just started up."

Lulu Yazzie has a problem—her first name is often misspelled, even by family members. Once, while we were interviewing her husband, and she was busy in the house cooking a late Sunday breakfast for the children, she called out the window to make sure we got it right: "My first name is Lulu. That's L-U-L-U!"

Opposite: Lulu Yazzie, *Rooster*, c. 1990. Carved and painted wood and cottonwood bark, 16" x 15" x 17".

The Yazzies live in a bungalow behind the home of Lulu Yazzie's father and mother, Woody and Anne Herbert, and they are the proud possessors of a gasoline-operated electric generator. "We run the generator four hours a day in the evening." According to Lulu, this procedure enables "the five children to have light to do their homework, and we can all watch TV."

With the exception of the generator and assorted family vehicles, life here on the high ground above Sweetwater hasn't changed very much in the last hundred years. Their pickup trucks make attending squaw dances (formerly ceremonial, now social in nature) in summer and Yeibichai dances after the first frost in winter much easier, but the main cash crop is still wool. However, the men seem to keep busy; Wilford Yazzie and Woody Herbert are usually away from home at one function or another whenever we come to call.

Lulu Yazzie helped her husband from the very beginning, but her signature work—carved roosters, chickens, skunks, and cats—wasn't undertaken until the late 1980s. Like the rest of the family, Lulu Yazzie carves cottonwood with a hatchet and various wood-gouging chisels. Her creations are brightly decorated caricatures of animals. Her art is less serious in intent, and perhaps less creative, than that of her husband or father, but Yazzie's keen sense of humor permeates the sculpture. "It's easy to sell to museum gift shops and galleries," explains Indian trader Jack Beasley. "You don't have to be a serious collector to want to display one of Lulu's delightful animals in your home. And who else would think of using the inner bark of the cottonwood tree to make a rooster's tail feathers!"

Wilford Yazzie, by contrast, is very serious in his approach to sculpture. "When I got time," he proclaims, "I make the things I see about me. I just take up a hatchet and make 'em." The animal that brought Yazzie his initial fame in the early 1980s was the black scavenger, the crow. His crows have fierce brass tack eyes and the threatening look of savage birds that movie director Alfred Hitchcock portrayed some years ago. Sometimes, Yazzie makes crow couples, a mother and father guarding their young in a nest of bark or just standing alone as though perched and ready to fly.

Yazzie is known for an assortment of other animals—goats, cows, and even dragons. "Sometimes I'll make a few Yeibichai dancers," he boasts, "but I made the crows first. Woody makes 'em now, but mine are better."

Wilford Yazzie, *Crows*, c. 1988. Mixed media (carved and painted cottonwood, bark, beer tabs, and tack eyes), 11" x 24" x 12".

Tom Yazzie

Tom Yazzie glances out at the vista in front of his yard/auto repair shop and says: "Look at that big rock over there. That's Black Rock, we look at it every day. My grandfather, Frank Stewart, saved that rock from being blown to powder in 1955. The state of Arizona made a saddle in that rock and was going to destroy the whole thing for a highway. But Stewart organized the community and stopped them."

The reservation experiences of Tom Yazzie's generation are hard for us to understand today. "I was born in 1930, in Fort Defiance, and school was different then," he explains. "We boys went to the boarding school in Defiance until someone noticed that we needed to shave. After I began to shave, they said 'you graduated from eighth grade; go into the Army.' So I went—from about 1947 to 1954."

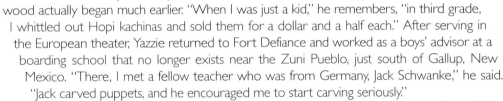

Yazzie served in Europe and has stated that he used his spare time to carve with his Army-issue bayonet.[4] But his love affair with shaping wood actually began much earlier. "When I was just a kid," he remembers, "in third grade, I whittled out Hopi kachinas and sold them for a dollar and a half each." After serving in the European theater, Yazzie returned to Fort Defiance and worked as a boys' advisor at a boarding school that no longer exists near the Zuni Pueblo, just south of Gallup, New Mexico. "There, I met a fellow teacher who was from Germany, Jack Schwanke," he said. "Jack carved puppets, and he encouraged me to start carving seriously."

There never was any doubt as to what the subject matter of Yazzie's work would be— Navajo daily and ceremonial life. "My brother, Alfred Yazzie, is a famous medicine man," he states with pride. "I attend all of the ceremonies, often spend the whole night watching my brother. Then, I carve them as they are. If they're right, Alfred tells me—'pretty close, Tom.' I have even recreated ceremonies they don't do any more, like the bear dance."

Yazzie and his wife, Marie Prea, have five girls and three boys. Marie Yazzie is a well-known ceramicist, who makes decorative bowls and some clay sculpture, depicting Indian figures in rather heroic poses. In addition to his art, Tom Yazzie is occupied with many other pursuits. He runs a one-man repair shop for cars, trucks, and farm implements, rents himself out with a red tractor he owns to do farm work, and loves to drive a 1957 Willis Jeep off into the back country to fish. "But when the corn is harvested," he says, "I can really do a lot of good carving."

Yazzie, like so many other carvers, uses the root of the cottonwood tree and simple, hand-held implements. He has made some single figures, but he is probably best known for his sets of two or more Navajos (generally about twelve inches in height), depicting his generation in realistic daily activity or participating in ceremonies. The birth of Jesus is not generally celebrated as part of the Navajo religion, but Yazzie has made an occasional Nativity scene. "A little Christianity can't hurt," he explains, "and our family does observe Christmas." These Nativities are also of great interest because the participants—shepherds, Mary, Joseph, etc.—are Navajo, dressed in Navajo attire. Wrapped in trade blankets, the figures wear their hair in the Navajo bun and are adorned with Navajo squash blossom necklaces and concho belts.

Yazzie is a specialist in capturing small details of everyday costume and dress. In his earliest work, he added found objects—feathers and bits of stone. But his skill has progressed to a point where he currently carves most of these small details (belts, feathers, and various decorations) from wood. Yazzie works very hard to achieve realism. His dance sets, for instance, are accurate in every detail and almost to scale. Yazzie's art is all the more valuable because he has successfully preserved and recorded a generation of Navajo traditional life that is in danger of disappearing.

Opposite: Tom Yazzie, *Navajo Couple,* c. 1991. Carved and painted cottonwood, 10" x 6 ¹/₂" x 3".

Yazzie's first major Yeibichai dance set, completed in 1957 or 1958, brought him instant recognition.[5] This set, which includes masked dancers, medicine man, and patient, is now in the collection of the Navajo Nation Museum in Window Rock. Tom Yazzie has received many awards at Native American art exhibits throughout the Southwest, and he has been widely exhibited and collected both in this country and abroad.

Notes to Central Region

1 Many Navajos who own livestock have several hogans as the animals must be moved from place to place during various seasons. Other Navajos move to a cooler place in summer, a simpler hogan, often similar to a brush arbor. In some instances, summer hogans are constructed on the same property as the principal residence—meals are taken there and family members may also sleep in the summer hogan.

2 Andrew Tsihnahjinnie has spelled his name at least five different ways. The spelling used here is the one used by the artist to sign his later paintings. Andrew's son, Tsosie, prefers the early, simpler spelling "Tsinajinnie" and plans to formally change his name to Tsinajinnie. Most of the information in this article was obtained in separate interviews with Andrew Tsihnahjinnie and with his son Tsosie at the family home in Rough Rock, Arizona.

3 Few records exist prior to 1928, the date the Navajo Tribe commenced a formal program of record maintenance.

4 Guy and Doris Mothan, *Naciementos* (Flagstaff: Northland Press, 1979), 52-54.

5 The original reaction to Yazzie's Yei carvings by older medicine men was "no good." They predicted Yazzie would go blind. After a few years, no harm befalling Yazzie, the carvings were accepted. See Nancy J. Parezo, *Navajo Sandpainting from Religious Act to Commercial Art* (Tucson: University of Arizona Press, 1983).

THE WESTERN REGION

The artists of the western region work primarily with wool and clay, traditional materials for the Navajo. But each artist in his or her own way has broken with the community ties that required a certain amount of conformity—based on custom, tradition, and taboos—and is making unique, even revolutionary, art.

Flagstaff, Arizona, is a hill-hugging, Midwestern-appearing town that follows along the rail-yards of the Santa Fe Railroad. People vacation here in summer to escape the heat of Phoenix and in winter to ski. It is the gateway to the Grand Canyon, Lake Powell, Monument Valley, and the Indian country to the north. And wherever you go, look up. The San Francisco Peaks are an ever-present reminder that this is the western boundary of the Dinétah. This beautiful mountain range, covered with ponderosa pine and snow-capped in winter, is sacred to the Navajo and to their Hopi neighbors.

On U.S. 180 toward Grand Canyon, there's an important museum for Native American enthusiasts. The Museum of Northern Arizona occupies a grouping of indigenous wood and stone buildings that display works by some of the artists in this book—as well as other well-known and emerging Native American artists. Many are prize winners who have been invit-

ed to the museum to demonstrate and show their art over the years. The Museum of Northern Arizona's three summer shows (Zuni around Memorial Day weekend, Hopi near the Fourth of July, and the Navajo show about the last weekend in July) are must-stops for collectors. These shows have been instrumental in helping to stimulate innovation among Navajo artists. The museum maintains a serious gift shop for collectors and casual browsers alike, specializing in Zuni, Hopi, and Navajo art. Several of the objects pictured in this book were purchased at the Museum of Northern Arizona shop from Steve Pickle, its manager.

About thirty miles north of Flagstaff, and still in the shadow of the San Francisco Peaks, is the trading post at Sacred Mountain, owned by Bill Beaver. The sign on the white, weathered trad-

Bill Beaver at his Sacred Mountain trading post, founded circa 1915. Beaver wholesales the work of the Shonto/Cow Springs potters throughout the United States.

ing post on U.S. Route 89 reads "Sacred Mountain," and just below, *"Dook'o'oosłíd Naalghehe Bahogan"* ("West Mountain—House of Merchandise").

Beaver's post, though part of the checkerboard that is a short distance off the reservation, is in the shadow of what the Navajo refer to as Sacred Mountain, the western mountain of the Dinétah. It is one of the Southwest's historic trading posts, founded circa 1915.

Busloads of multi-national tourists on their rapid journey between sites such as Flagstaff, Grand Canyon, Page, and Monument Valley don't stop here. "I won't even build 'em a parking lot," declares Beaver. Bill Beaver was the first trader to collect, promote, and sell contemporary Navajo folk pottery. "Before I came along, they [other traders] scoffed at it—called it mud."

Today, Bill Beaver wholesales the work of the Shonto/Cow Springs potters throughout the United States—galleries, collectors, and museums place orders by phone, but tourists still just drive by. Beaver likes it "the way it is." He sells craft items and convenience foods to the Indians and enjoys our good long talks on a slow Sunday morning.

The tourist buses are parked many deep at the post at Cameron. This is a historic post, once on the wagon road from Flagstaff to Lee's Ferry, a short drive to the north of Sacred Mountain. In 1916, after a new bridge was built, Hubert Richardson built a trading post near the west end of the bridge. The post prospered; a hotel, café, and gas pumps joined the original facilities. Cameron Trading Post has long been an important stopoff for travelers.

Cameron carries a wide assortment of rugs (some are labeled "Made in Mexico"), jewelry, and Navajo pottery. Although a large portion of the post's merchandise is tourist-oriented, top-of-the-line items are also carried, many of them in a separate structure, a gallery, that is opened for serious collectors upon request.

North of Cameron you are back in our kind of Indian Country—following the rise of the Colorado River towards its source. At Tuba City, which is named after the Hopi Indian chief, called Tivi or Tuba, there is a marker erected by the Mormons referring to the chief as a member of the Water and Corn Clan. He served as a scout for Kit Carson's expedition in 1865 and was a friend of the Mormons, granting them rights to establish a settlement in Hopi country.

Three major Indian Country roads intersect at, or near, Tuba City—U.S. 89 and 160 and Arizona State Highway 264. Historically, the area was settled by the Mormons in the late 1870s. However, the Mormon settlers had to sell their land to the federal government in 1902–1903, when it was determined they had built on Navajo land. One of those dispossessed was Joseph Lehi Foutz, the patriarch of a large Mormon family.

Foutz settled in the Fruitland area. Six of his thirteen sons became Indian traders; the family is still active in trading today in Farmington and Shiprock (see page 68).

The Tuba City Trading Post, the oldest on the reservation, dates from 1870 and appears today much as it looked in the early 1900s—an octagonal, hoganlike design of gray limestone with clerestory windows. (Rehabilitation in the late 1980s restored the post to its original appearance, reversing the impact of an unfortunate remodeling in 1955.) Theodore Roosevelt visited the post, and today, tourists clad in shorts are usually present buying Indian-made objects.

The post at Tuba City no longer performs its original function of supplying the Indians with staples and clothing. During modern times, it has specialized in convenience foods, VCR movies, and tourist items. The post has become primarily a center for the display and sale of Native American arts and crafts, principally fine rugs and jewelry.

The "Golden Arches" of McDonald's can be seen in the shadow of the post; it fills the stomachs of tourists and natives alike. However, we have discovered that you can get a wonderful picante Navajo taco down the street at Poncho's.

On the north side of the main Tuba City intersection, there is a perpetual Navajo "swap meet," which is particularly active on Friday afternoons. Hay, used tools, clothing, and sheep are some of the items offered. In the past, you'd also find grilled mutton and green chile on a skewer. In the mid-1980s, we also found potters like Louise Goodman, Lorena Bartlett, and Faye Tso there, selling and trading utilitarian ware. We bought coffee pots, casseroles, and even frying pans made from clay (pictured below). All can be used.

The grilled mutton is gone now from the "swap meet," and so are the potters. In fact, I doubt if a utilitarian clay pot can be found for sale anywhere within the Navajo Nation. When we show them to museum curators, they put well-manicured fingers across their chins and intone: "Uhh! Ummm!—Interesting." But there is uniform enthusiasm for the most innovative contemporary pottery by many of the same artists, and you wouldn't have had the one without the other.

Once you become hooked on Navajo pottery, a visit to the Shonto/Cow Springs area will become a compulsion. The intersection of U.S. 160 and Arizona Route 98 is referred to locally as the "Shonto Corner." It is roughly in the center of the area in which most Navajo pottery has always been

Louise Rose Goodman, Lorena Bartlett, and Faye Tso, traditional Navajo cooking pots, c. 1985. Fired clay and piñon pitch; frying pan (Goodman), 2" x 10 1/2" x 13 1/2"; coffee pot (Bartlett), 9 1/2" x 7" x 4"; casserole (Tso), 9 1/2" x 10 1/2" x 6 3/4".

made. Black Mesa, a traditional source for Navajo clay, is a foreboding presence above the "Corner." The Peabody Coal Company has a lease at Black Mesa and is currently mining coal there for use at the Navajo Power Plant below the Glen Canyon Dam at Page, Arizona; an electric railroad runs alongside the road, bringing to mind the lyrics of John Prine's 1970s hit song "Paradise": "Mr. Peabody's coal train has hauled it [Black Mesa] away."

If you drive down the almost-vertical red sand road into the canyon, you'll find the Shonto Trading Post—a bustling, historic gem located on the floor of Shonto Canyon. Its appeal is enhanced by the magnificent cottonwoods that surround it. The enterprise was founded in 1915 by John Wetherill and Joe Lee; supplies were initially sold out of a tent. Permanent buildings were erected shortly after World War I, and the post was eventually taken over by the Carson family. The last member of the Carson family to manage the post was Raymond Drolet, grandson of the pioneering trader, O.J. (Stokes) Carson. In mid-1992, Raymond and his wife, Melissa, leased the operation to Al and Margaret Grieve. The post is still a traditional one with a large dry-goods section; jeans, blouses, shoes, baby clothes, leather, and saddle tack—all are carried at Shonto. Since the nearest bank is at Page about sixty miles away, the trading post performs some of the customary functions, now dying out at other posts, such as cashing checks and providing credit. Also, customers receive mail-order purchases and UPS deliveries at the Shonto post.

The Shonto Trading Post was founded in 1915 and was originally operated out of a tent. The buildings at the post were erected shortly after World War I.

Shonto's customers are almost entirely Navajo—women wearing the traditional long, velvet skirts and blouses, adorned in turquoise and silver, and men in hats, western flannel shirts, and boots.

Unfortunately, Shonto Trading Post specialized in rugs and never carried much pottery. (Although the Shonto area is not known for the quality of its rugs, almost all the women in the area do some weaving.) However, the new trader, Al Grieve, has pledged not to be outbid and "to buy the very best of the innovative pottery. Alice Cling has an account here," said Grieve, "but can you imagine—the former operators [though successful traders] never bought one of her pots."

The general area near Shonto/Cow Springs is probably second only to Grand Canyon in tourism. Monument Valley and Navajo National Monument are must-sees for their archae-ological sites, monolithic geological wonders, and sunsets beyond compare. But the mag-net that has drawn us to this area is Navajo pottery. A typical Navajo pot, made accord-ing to the dictates of tradition and taboo, was once considered interesting only to the anthropologist. But pottery has long been part of traditional Navajo life. According to Navajo beliefs, pottery was one of the crafts learned from the Holy People. In addition, many Navajo ceremonies mention "pots" or "bowls."

Pottery making has conventionally been considered "women's work." There was noth-ing to prevent a man from working in clay, but if he did so, he might be looked on with disfavor. Perhaps one of the reasons that potting came to be considered women's work is that they attended to the food preparation chores. Pottery was not considered a decora-tive element in the home or hogan. Its functions were associated with ceremonial prac-tices and utilitarian use. As a result, all Navajo pottery looked very similar, and the artistry of the individual maker was lost. One bean pot looked and functioned like every other bean pot, and the same was true for coffee pots, frying pans, and even drum pots.

Clay in the western region is taken from places like Black Mesa, the landmark towering over Cow Springs and the Shonto Corner. After the clay is properly mixed (some potters add potsherds as a temper, others use volcanic cinders), impurities are sifted out. Then, coils are formed and wound upward until the desired shape and size is achieved. The ves-sel is then smoothed with a burnished corncob (recently, some potters are using river stones or Popsicle sticks) both inside and outside. Tradition allows only one decorative element to be added to the pot—a beaded necklace just below the rim called a *biyo'*.

Once the preliminary work is finished, the pot is set outdoors in the sun or near a hot stove to dry before firing. While cedar is the preferred fuel, almost any type of fire-hold-ing device can be employed as a kiln. Fireplaces, wood-burning stoves, and open pits are all used. Each of these methods will produce "fire clouds." These black or blackish-gray discolorations appear when wood oxidizes and ash comes in contact with the clay.

When the pot has been allowed to cool, melted piñon pitch is applied to all of its sur-faces. The pitch is kept in a tin can heating near a fire, its contents melted golden brown. Two sticks are needed to apply pitch; the end of one is wrapped in a rag dipped in pitch and the other is inserted into the vessel, to hold it while pitch is rubbed on. Once the pitch has hardened, the pot is watertight. If a pot is used for cooking, there is a noticeable, but not unpleasant, residual pitch flavor.

Pots destined for use in ceremonies are made in the same manner but may require a special blessing by a medicine man. One of the most interesting is the drum pot. These pots vary in size and are covered with a deerskin. Two holes, called "eyes," are then punched into the skin. Water poured into these pots through the "eyes" achieves the desired resonance.

Navajo pottery had its place within the Dinétah. It was cheaper than the tin, plastic, and iron ware available at the local posts. The women could swap it with each other. But these advantages slowly disappeared. Commercial cookery became more available, and the women could use their time for other pursuits. Then, just as it appeared that Navajo pottery would disappear entirely (except for a small output for ceremonial purposes), a few of the artists began to innovate—adding their personal artistic endeavors to the work. Several traders, like Bill Beaver, who had been collecting Navajo pottery right along, began to buy and sell the more innovative work in the 1960s. By 1980, there was a resurgence in Navajo pottery making, and it was recognized as a "new" art form—collected and exhibited from coast to coast.

Myra Tso Kaye, *Ram Pot*, 1992. Fired clay and piñon pitch, 15" height x 29 1/2" circumference.

It was fascinating for us to witness this rapid transition, from utilitarian "mud" to art pottery. In recent years, as the ware lost its utilitarian purposes, the potters slowly began to realize that they were potting for a different and distant market that sought their work for its artistic merit. By the 1990s, artists such as Alice Cling, Christine McHorse, and Lorraine Williams began attending fairs, powwows, and the Santa Fe Indian Market, competing for ribbons and prizes in these events. Although the pottery was still made in the traditional Navajo manner, the new designs and styles that emerged more closely resembled art objects.

Stars were born overnight. Betty Manygoats, Chris McHorse, and Faye Tso were exhibited throughout the country in the traveling exhibition, *The Cutting Edge: Contemporary Folk Art from the Rosenak Collection.* Chris McHorse, Alice Cling, Jimmy Wilson, Faye Tso, and Lucy Leuppe McKelvey all won ribbons at the Indian Market. Only a few years ago, Navajo pottery wasn't even a category at the market. Today, pots by the superstars command prices ranging upwards to ten thousand dollars.

{ Above: Florence Riggs (right) and her mother, Louise Nez, weave on an unusual double loom, designed by Louise's son, Bill.
Opposite: Louise Nez, *Reservation Scene,* 1992. A more traditional pictorial rug, commercial yarn, 38 1/2" x 42 1/2".

Our search for pictorial weavers in the western region took us to Tuba City, The Gap/Bitter Springs, and Echo Cliffs. In these relatively isolated places, we found weavers that dared to be different—and rugs we could call art.

There are examples of pictorial weaving by the Navajos as early as the 1860s. Of particular renown is a Chief White Antelope blanket, now in the collection of the School of American Research in Santa Fe. This blanket, recovered after the Sand Creek Massacre in 1864, incorporates four small ducks into a geometric design. While there are a few other examples of early pictorial weaving, including a blanket with a cow pattern that was probably woven in the 1880s, pictorial images were not widespread until almost the end of the nineteenth century. By that time, trading posts were spreading to new areas, and the railroad had become a reality.

Other noted early pictorial weavings were done by Hastiin Klah ("Lefthanded"), who permanently preserved a number of sandpaintings in Navajo weavings. Klah was one of the most famous medicine men of his time. Because of belief in his powers, Klah was able to record sandpaintings without harm to himself or his viewers. He persuaded Mary Cabot Wheelwright to finance a Museum of Navajo Ceremonial Art in Santa Fe (now the Wheelwright Museum of the American Indian). About eighteen of Hastiin Klah's seventy sandpainting weavings (some as large as 105" by 115"), completed between 1919 and Klah's death in 1937, are today in the collection of the Wheelwright Museum.[1] Other Klah weavings are in institutions such as the Museum of Northern Arizona.

Nevertheless, pictorial textiles have always represented a very small percentage of Navajo weavings. Some estimates indicate that pictorials generally comprise less than one percent of the total.[2] Our informal survey confirms an estimate in this range. Bill Malone, Hubbell Trading Post, for instance, stated that there may be several thousand Navajo weaving traditional rugs, while there are only about two dozen serious pictorial weavers (excluding weavers who make one or two pictorials and others who make very small tourist-type rugs like the Tree of Life).

Although traders usually consider pictorials a "slow-seller," these rugs enjoyed a brief period of popularity during the 1960s and 1970s. A 1975–1976 show of pictorials at the Museum of International Folk Art featured rugs (primarily from this period) showing reservation landscapes, patriotic themes, and holiday designs.

Subsequently, pictorials became hard to find, with the exception of very small rugs intended for tourists rather than collectors. Those that did turn up were, for the most part, not innovative. Reservation scenes were oft-repeated, as were rugs with eagles or flag motifs. Many of the rugs were woven in the Chinle–Many Farms area, which has long been known for pictorial weaving.

We started our research in that area of the reservation. However, to our surprise, the most innovative weavers of this decade live along U.S. 89 between Tuba City and Page, especially between The Gap and Bitter Springs. Another weaver was found in Tall Mountain, not far from Shonto, and the Pete sisters live near Carson (an unlikely location since that trading post has changed hands and has not been purchasing rugs for some time, though that situation is beginning to change too).

The pictorial phenomenon is difficult to explain. Sometimes, a family member starts making this type of rug, and others follow. Often, it is based on individual vision. Several weavers told us they find pictorials "more interesting to make" than traditional patterns. Linda

Nez (see page 140) says that one of her reasons for making pictorials, in addition to the precedent set by her aunt and mother, is that "there must be more than a thousand women out there doing traditional weaving, while less than thirty are weaving pictorials."

Traders can also play a role. Notah Dineh in Cortez is an example. The Leighton brothers (Gregg and Glenn) at this post buy all the really fine and innovative pictorials that are brought into the store. A number of other trading posts in Shiprock, Farmington, Ganado, and Chinle are following the growing renewal of interest in pictorials and purchasing major rugs. This in turn encourages the weavers. Since a large pictorial can take four to six months to complete, a reasonable market is important. (The majority of the pictorial weavers we interviewed can make traditional rugs but choose not to; the methods used for weaving both types are the same.)

The drive north on U.S. 89 from the intersection of U.S. 160 leading to Tuba City is through a land of great rugged beauty. The road rises toward the headwaters of the majestic Colorado River. But the isolation of the area and its Navajo inhabitants cannot be absorbed unless you venture off the paved highway.

The Gap Trading Post, established about 1880 at the foot of Echo Cliffs near Hamblin Wash, is a one-story, rectangular building built out of blocks of locally quarried red sandstone. It still

Betty Manygoats, *Bull*, c. 1988.
Fired clay and piñon pitch,
4" x 5 1/2" x 2 1/2".

functions as the center of commerce for the entire area; animal feed, dry goods, and food staples may all be purchased here. The only public telephone between Page and Tuba City, a distance of almost one hundred miles, is located at The Gap. "But," says Kathy Troglia, the store's manager, "no matter how many times we fix it, it never works. If we had a real emergency, I don't know what we'd do."

The Gap carries a fairly large supply of locally woven pictorial rugs. However, Troglia informed us: "I can only sell small rugs to tourists—the smaller the better—and birds or Trees of Life are the most popular." Not what we were looking for.

The Gap was the jumping-off place for an old wagon road, which tortuously finds its way through the rugged red sandstone of Echo Cliffs toward Copper Mine and on up north to Page. We traveled the old road hoping for a picture, but the Arizona Electric Power Company has obscured the view behind giant steel towers and high power lines.

In the near future, there will be other signs of modernization at the old post. Thriftway has been negotiating with the Navajo for six years to acquire the lease.

Bitter Springs is about twenty-six miles north of The Gap. Its feature attraction is a small cluster of houses next to the highway under Echo Cliffs.

Linda Nez, Susie Black, Frances Sampson, and Sara Tso live and work in this area. Kathy Troglia at The Gap may instruct them to "weave small," but they ignore her.

A good route south is through Second Mesa (the Hopi Reservation) and Keams Canyon. While Hopi is not part of our western region, Keams Canyon is. The traders there maintain an important inventory of contemporary Hopi and Navajo folk art, jewelry, and kachinas. Several artists in this book, including Faye and Emmett Tso, Myra Tso Kaye, and Ida Sahmie, are represented in the Keams Canyon Arts and Craft Gallery upstairs from the cafeteria—a fun place to shop.

There has been a trading post at Keams Canyon, Arizona, since 1875 when Thomas Keam was licensed

Faye Tso, *Head of Emmett*, c. 1986. Fired clay (inverted bean pot), with piñon pitch, 14" height x 31" circumference.

120

to open a post in the canyon that today bears his name. The present grouping of buildings (gas station, arts and craft gallery, restaurant, grocery store, and motel) is located off Arizona Route 264. The Navajo and Hopi are sometimes uneasy neighbors, but both tribes are welcome here, and this is one reason the post is so unique.

Bruce and Ron McGee are the children of Cliff (C. F.) McGee who, with his brother William, purchased the trading post from Juan Lorenzo Hubbell in 1938. While Cliff McGee is still alive and involved, the second generation has pretty much taken over the day-to-day operation.

Trading is in Bruce McGee's blood, and he was one of the first to recognize the significance of contemporary Navajo pottery. McGee reminisces about the day of his discovery as follows: "Faye Tso came into the post one day in 1974 with several large pots appliquéd with corn and Yei figures. Before that, all we saw from the Navajo were dark, bulky, mud pots—good to drink from if you didn't mind the flavor of pitch. There was a worldwide market for Hopi pots at that time, but you couldn't sell one that was Navajo made. With the discovery of Faye Tso, the Navajo became competitive."

Bruce McGee also recognized the importance of Ida Sahmie. "Ida lived at Low Mountain," he says, "when she started bringing in pots during the 1980s. She had learned to pot from her Hopi mother-in-law, Priscilla Namingha. Here was a Navajo, innovating on Hopi-like pottery but depicting her own culture [Yei designs, etc.]. Sahmie's pots sold immediately and for more money than the Hopi potters of her generation."

Today, Bruce McGee's principal business is retailing and wholesaling the rugs, jewelry, pottery, and sandpaintings of the Navajo and Hopi from his modern gallery in Holbrook, Arizona. "The reservation now is surrounded by chain stores like Wal-Mart and K-Mart," he sadly relates. "The day of the old trading post is mostly dead; we don't trade; we no longer act as a go-between with the government; we don't take much pawn; we don't extend credit; and the Indians have wheels."

Bruce McGee's refrain may foretell the future, but for now, the link between Indian trader and Navajo artist is essential. When the people speak, the first ear to hear will usually be that of a perceptive trader, like Bruce McGee.

Silas and Bertha Claw

Silas and Bertha Claw have broken with Navajo pottery tradition and the customs of their Shonto/Cow Springs region. Although their forms are more or less traditional, the Claws appliqué colorful pictorial designs onto their vessels.

Silas Claw was born on December 15, 1913, but on most days he still mounts a skittish white horse and rides out to herd sheep and goats. When we photographed him recently, his horse reared each time the flash popped. The next day, the seventy-eight year old herder was limping.

"Horse throw you?" I asked. "Yah-Yup," he replied, and that's about all the English you'll get out of Claw.

The Claws live on a dirt track overlooking the Shonto Corner. A big, red rooster that family members describe as "mean" hangs out under their front porch. They also maintain a plywood hogan that has been converted into a pottery studio/guest house. Now that Silas and Bertha have aged a bit and their eyes aren't what they used to be, two nieces, Daisy Tate and Ella Shortman, work in the hogan, helping to paint and sand the ware.

About 1968, Silas Claw began to work in clay even though pottery making, like basket making, is considered women's work. Bertha Claw assisted him from the very beginning, and it is difficult to differentiate their pots or tell exactly who does what. However, their combined style is instantly recognizable and has evolved over the years. The earliest ware was appliquéd, unpainted, and unsigned. Presently, the pots are signed "S.B. Claw," and the appliqué and some decorative elements are painted with acrylics. The forms are fairly traditional—single-, two-, and even multi-spouted vessels—but the appliqué and design motifs are highly unusual: hogans, herders, bears, goats, cats, even tepees. On occasion, the Claws will paint the background of the pottery, as well as the appliquéd portions. This is unusual in that western Navajos, including potters of the Shonto/Cow Springs area, do not paint designs on pottery because they believe that such painted designs can

Right: Silas and Bertha Claw, *Bear and Ram Pipes* and *Necklace,* c. 1988. Fired clay, shellac, and acrylic paint; pipes, 2 1/4" x 4 1/2" x 2 1/2" each; necklace (clay beads), 14" in length. Opposite: Two wedding vases and one triple-spouted vase, c. 1987-1988. Fired clay, shellac, and acrylic paint, 8 1/4" height x 15 1/4" circumference each.

cause natural disasters. Silas and Bertha also depart from tradition by sealing their work with shellac, rather than the traditional piñon pitch, to keep the paint from running.

In addition to their pots, the Claws are also known for their necklaces of strung clay beads (birds and arrowheads), decorated pipes, animals, and small, painted figures of Navajo men and women. Recently, Silas has even created a few tableaus, such as Indian cowboys bulldogging a steer. Silas and Bertha Claw have been widely exhibited and have won numerous ribbons throughout the Southwest. They were among the first innovative potters to be shown by Bill Beaver at the Sacred Mountain Trading Post and today are among the most popular of the contemporary Navajo potters.

Alice Cling

Alice Cling looked at her pots in 1976 and said to herself, "Alice, they are ugly!"

"So," she adds, "I shaped and polished some to make them beautiful." This bit of soul searching by the young artist helped revolutionize contemporary Navajo pottery.

Cling broke with tradition dictating the shape of the vessel—cooking pots, water storage jars, cups, water bottles or canteens, bowls, pipes, and ceremonial drum pots—and developed her own graceful, beautifully shaped forms. Tradition also called for a decorative fillet around the rim, a *biyo'*, with a small break similar to the break in Navajo baskets. This *atiin* is "the way out" for the spirit. Alice Cling discarded this tradition, too. Some of her pots contain no biyo'; others contain a biyo' so stylized that it merely suggests a fillet. Cling's highly polished decorative ware was an instant success at Bill Beaver's Sacred Mountain Trading Post.

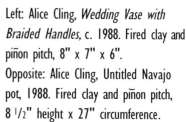

Left: Alice Cling, *Wedding Vase with Braided Handles*, c. 1988. Fired clay and piñon pitch, 8" x 7" x 6".
Opposite: Alice Cling, Untitled Navajo pot, 1988. Fired clay and piñon pitch, 8 1/2" height x 27" circumference.

In other senses, however, Alice has remained true to Navajo pottery traditions. "I won't use a wheel, and I cannot bring myself to add much decoration because Grandmother said that would be bad," Cling declares. (Navajo potters have long believed that excessive decoration is wrong, that it can bring bad luck or physical calamities such as earthquakes or storms.)

Alice Cling, who was born on March 21, 1946, lives across U.S. 160 from her mother, Rose Williams, in a stucco tract house built by HUD. "Someday," she says, "we'll build a house of our own on the hill in back of Mother." She graduated from Intermountain Indian School (a high school no longer in existence) in Brigham City, Utah. Since 1969, Cling has held a position as a teacher's aide at the Shonto Boarding School. Every year, she threatens to quit and take up pottery full time, but in the summer of 1992, she finally admitted to us: "I guess I like my job even though I can now make a good living in pottery."

The pots are formed, sanded, polished, covered with pitch, and dried on a wood-burning stove in the Clings' small living/dining/recreation room. But the crucial firing is usually done outside, across the highway, under the watchful eye of her mother, a more traditional potter.

Cling gets her unique and beautiful leatherlike finish from a red clay slip Bill Beaver acquires in trade from the Walapai Indians. According to Beaver, the exact location of this clay is a well-kept secret, and he says, "I'll only supply Alice with it. An Alice Cling pot is something very special."

Cling is credited with being the first contemporary Navajo to polish her ware with a smooth, well-worn river stone instead of the traditional burnished corn cob. To obliterate the dimpled effect caused by pressure from the potter's fingers as she (or, increasingly, he) works, Navajo potters usually use a piece of corn cob that has been singed in fire to prevent it from too severely abrading the vessel's surface. Small pieces of gourd are also commonly used for scraping and polishing.

Before firing, Cling polishes her pots to a high gloss. This gives her pottery a distinctive sheen after the piñon pitch is applied. She then uses waxed paper to wipe off excess pitch. The pottery of Alice Cling is so stylized and unique that some consider her work to be "fine art." While a Cling pot does not have the folk sensibility of a Manygoats horny toad pot or a Goodman bear, for example, it is, nonetheless, folk art by the criteria we outlined earlier. Cling has had no formal training. She has independently developed a style that reflects her individual vision and works by hand under very primitive conditions—far more primitive than the Southern folk potters who use motor-driven wheels. In the end, all great folk artists create "art," thus occasionally blurring the line between folk art and fine art.

In the past two or three years, Cling has for the most part limited her production to small pots in forms she has made previously, a typical result of fame and the accompanying ability to sell everything as fast as it is dry. Pots signed "Alice" (or, on earlier work, "Alice Cling" or simply "AC") are among the most sought-after southwestern pottery. We recently saw a small one sell at auction for more than a thousand dollars. Cling has won numerous awards for Native American pottery and at her first appearance at Indian Market in 1989 took home a prestigious blue ribbon.

125

Louise Rose Goodman

Louise Goodman, who was born on Christmas day in 1937, is one of the transitional folk artists, those whose work lies somewhere between traditional pottery and the art pottery that was to follow. She was among the first to realize that the demand for her utilitarian ware had come to an end and that something had to be done to save the art form. Goodman was also "one of the ladies" to follow Bill Beaver from Shonto to Sacred Mountain. "I talked to Beaver and later to Jan Musial and Jan Bell," she relates, "and they said 'make something different.' So I did and I brought 'em to Bill Beaver, and the things that sold—I made 'em back [repeated popular items so that Beaver could keep them in stock]."

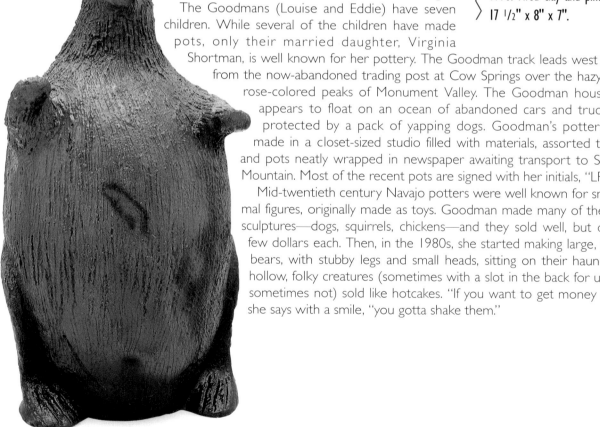

Left: Louise Rose Goodman, *Bear*, 1990. Fired clay and piñon pitch, 17 ¹/₂" x 8" x 7".

The Goodmans (Louise and Eddie) have seven children. While several of the children have made pots, only their married daughter, Virginia Shortman, is well known for her pottery. The Goodman track leads west from the now-abandoned trading post at Cow Springs over the hazy, rose-colored peaks of Monument Valley. The Goodman house appears to float on an ocean of abandoned cars and trucks, protected by a pack of yapping dogs. Goodman's pottery is made in a closet-sized studio filled with materials, assorted tools, and pots neatly wrapped in newspaper awaiting transport to Sacred Mountain. Most of the recent pots are signed with her initials, "LRG."

Mid-twentieth century Navajo potters were well known for small animal figures, originally made as toys. Goodman made many of these small sculptures—dogs, squirrels, chickens—and they sold well, but only for a few dollars each. Then, in the 1980s, she started making large, pot-bellied bears, with stubby legs and small heads, sitting on their haunches. These hollow, folky creatures (sometimes with a slot in the back for use as a bank, sometimes not) sold like hotcakes. "If you want to get money out of them," she says with a smile, "you gotta shake them."

The bears are her best-known work, but Goodman's greatest contribution to Navajo pottery may be her elegantly coiled pots, smoothed only on the inside, rough on the outside, with beautiful fireclouds. The latter style is truly transitional between utilitarian ware, which could be used for cooking and food storage, and the art pottery of the next generation.

Goodman's pottery has been exhibited at the Museum of Northern Arizona in Flagstaff, The Heard Museum in Phoenix, the Wheelwright Museum of the American Indian in Santa Fe, and the Navajo Tribal Museum in Window Rock; it is included in the permanent collections of the Wheelwright, the Tribal Museum, and the Arizona State Museum at the University of Arizona in Tucson.

Louise Rose Goodman, *Coiled Pot*, c. 1986. Fired clay and piñon pitch, 15 1/2" height x 31" circumference.

Helen Greyeyes

Only "agile goats and Indian ponies" should attempt what has been "damned by many travelers as the steepest, roughest half-mile in the United States"—the road leading east and straight up the red-rock canyon from the Shonto Trading Post.[3] But that's the road Helen Greyeyes travels to shop and sell her rugs. It's the lifeline between the Navajo living in Tall Mountain and the rest of Arizona.

Opposite: Helen Greyeyes, *Mountain Lion*, 1992. Pictorial rug, commercial yarn, 36 1/2" x 26 1/2".

Helen Greyeyes, born in 1938, still wears her hair in the traditional Navajo bun tied with white yarn. She still wears the long, pleated velvet skirt and velvet blouse of the Navajo matron, cares for a herd of sheep and goats with the help of her dogs, and speaks only in Navajo (translated for us by her son, Hubert Greyeyes). But for some reason she can't explain, a voice from within told her to break with tradition—to weave pictures in wool very different from her usual traditional rugs and different from the more customary pictorials, which frequently depict Navajo landscapes or Trees of Life. Her inspirations come from illustrations in books and magazines she can't read, introduced into her home by her eight children.

Greyeyes has a well-deserved reputation as one of the most skilled weavers in Tall Mountain. She learned her craft many years ago, and for the first twenty years of her career, her rugs were traditional, dictated by the designs favored by the traders with whom she dealt. The traders pay the highest prices for rugs made out of pure handspun wool hand-dyed with natural vegetable dyes, and that is what she made. "But," she explained, "my animals do not produce enough wool for all my rugs, and so I buy yarn in Farmington and Shonto for some of the pictorials I have been making for the last four years or so."

Hubert Greyeyes partially explains his mother's motivation as follows: "Mother had quit weaving for a period of time, preferring instead to sell the wool, but during the recent recession, money became scarce and the price of wool fell. So, mother started up again, and now she is making about two rugs a month."[4]

On the day of our visit, Helen Greyeyes was seated on a chrome-plated kitchen chair in front of a handmade loom placed against a wall in her brush arbor. She was working on a traditional red and black eye-dazzler on order from a trader. Her occasional pictorials are quite different from the rug she was currently weaving. The colors are softer—more pastel—and the borders, which set off the work, contrast sharply with the central picture, as though they were intended as frames. The weaving itself is every bit as fine in the pictorials as in the traditional rugs, but the subject matter is startlingly different. Greyeyes makes unusual pictures (bronc-busting riders, mountain lions dominating a landscape) not generally seen in Navajo weaving.

Al Grieve, the Indian Trader at the Shonto Post, told us that he will buy anything that Helen Greyeyes brings into his post—pictorial or traditional. The rugs he can't sell at Shonto are wholesaled to the historic Hubbell Trading Post at Ganado, which is a must-stop for visitors to the Navajo Nation. Greyeyes' rugs are also carried by Foutz's Indian Room in Farmington, and they appear occasionally at galleries in Santa Fe and Phoenix.

Helen Greyeyes, *Bucking Bronc,* 1991.
Pictorial rug, commercial yarn,
32" x 26 1/2".

Myra Tso Kaye

"I played with clay as a little girl," Myra Tso Kaye remembers, "but somewhere along the way I became serious. When I work with the yellow and gray clay from Black Mesa, I get a spiritual high, and the high comes only at my mother's house in Tuba City and only when I'm working in the Navajo Way."

Born in Tuba City in 1961, it's no wonder that Myra Kaye has a strong attachment to Navajo tradition. Kaye's grandfather, Osteen Bil"ah, was a medicine man, and so

is her father, Emmett Tso, and brother Irving Tso. Her mother, Faye Tso, is a herbalist. "I was initiated and I danced in ceremonies by age seven or eight, wearing the flat, square, ground-turquoise pigmented female mask. Of course, once I married, I could no longer dance at sacred ceremonies."

Kaye graduated from Tuba City High School and is presently majoring in art at Northern Arizona University in Flagstaff. "But school has nothing to do with my art," she recently stated. "I started out in electronics and transferred to art only because it gave me time to pot. The university teaches technology—how to fire in a kiln, for instance. But the spiritual part is lost, and so I go home to Tuba City and work in the Navajo Way."

Right: Myra Tso Kaye, *Bean Pot*, Appliquéd Corn Design, 1988. Fired clay and piñon pitch, 10 1/2" height x 20" circumference.

When we first met Myra Kaye (who pots under the name Tso) in 1985, her ware was very similar to that of her mother. She appliquéd corn and Yei figures on pots that were more refined in style than her mother's but less original. Lately, however, something wonderful has happened. Kaye has broken away from the notion that a pot must maintain a functional purpose; instead, she has turned to almost pure sculpture to satisfy her spiritual and artistic needs.

The work at her home in Tuba City has paid off. In July of 1992, Myra Tso Kaye won a blue ribbon at the prestigious Navajo Artists' Exhibition at Flagstaff's Museum of Northern Arizona. The prize-winning pot has a ram sculpted on one of the spouts of a wedding vase with caveman-like drawings of rams incised on the body of the piece. "The ram," Kaye explains, "is very, very sacred in the Navajo religion. The ram is the only animal able to withstand lightning, and its horn, ground and mixed with tobacco, cures head injuries and mental disabilities. I have filled it with cornmeal so it will have something to eat. Even the medicine men felt my ram pot had great power."

131

Betty Manygoats

"Don't fool with a horny toad," a Navajo advises. "Left alone, they bring good luck; fooled with—bad." But Betty Manygoats has earned national acclaim by breaking this ancient taboo, which includes depicting horny toads (horned lizards, *na'ashǫ' dich' ízhii*—"my grandfather") on pottery.

Manygoats was born Betty Barlow on January 30, 1945, and was taught by her grandmother to make pottery in the dying days of the utilitarian industry centered around the Shonto Corner. Bill Beaver, the owner of the Sacred Mountain Trading Post, recalls his first meeting with Betty Manygoats as follows: "When I first met Betty around 1975, her pots were undistinguished. I sent her home and told her to try something different. I waited a bit, then, in 1978, she brought me one encrusted with horny toads. Now I had something great!"

Manygoats, the mother of one son and nine daughters, still lives near the Shonto Corner where she grew up. To reach her home, we had to traverse a sheep-nibbled field, following tracks that lead into and over washes, sometimes filled with rusting, stripped-down carcasses of abandoned vehicles. The extended family maintains several prefabricated houses, and their original hogan/brush arbor has been turned into a studio. It was here, sometimes firing in an open pit outside and sometimes in an old rusted-through woodstove, that we found the artist at work, making her now-famous horny toad wedding vases.

Right: Betty Manygoats, *Horned Toad Wedding Vase*, 1988. Fired clay and piñon pitch, appliqued horned toads, 24 ¹/₂" x 10" x 10".
Opposite: Betty Manygoats, *Horse*, 1986. Fired clay, piñon pitch, and beeweed, 5 ¹/₂" x 7" x 1 ³/₄".

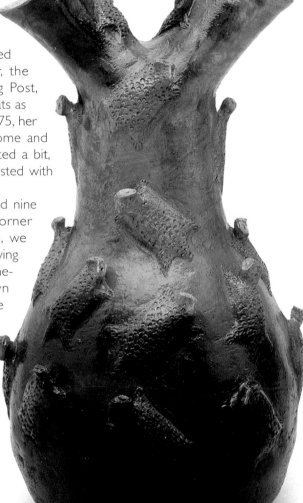

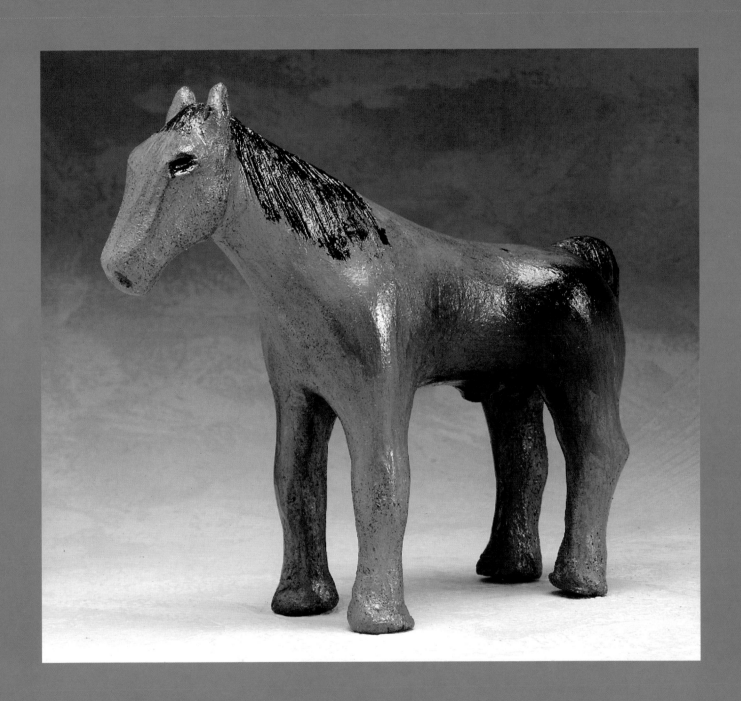

Manygoats does not negotiate in English, but some of her children will appear out of nowhere at the sight of a strange car, and they will strike a deal for a pot or two drying near the stove.

Manygoats' ware can be very large, heavy, double-spouted vessels, nearly three feet in height, but she also makes small, interestingly proportioned pots containing one or more horny toads. The smaller vessels are particularly popular in the galleries surrounding the reservation. The horny toads are appliquéd onto the pots, their scales carved out with a bobby pin. But several of Manygoats' children also make horny toad-encrusted pots. (Rita Manygoats is considered by many to be the most talented.) The work of the children is not nearly as valuable as the mother's. Fortunately, Manygoats signs her pots on the bottom—"BM" or "BBM" (Betty Barlow Manygoats). The children usually etch their own initials into the bottom of their work. During the last several years, Manygoats has not been as prolific as formerly; she seems content to supervise and instruct her children.

Manygoats is also known for her small renditions of animals—horses, cows, buffaloes—similar to the toys once given to Navajo children. Her husband, William Manygoats, also a potter, is another taboo breaker. The craft of pottery making, as well as basket making, was traditionally forbidden to men since it is considered entirely a woman's task. (Some Navajos believe that if a man makes a pot or basket, he may become impotent.) As a result, few men pot. William Manygoats makes round, heavy, colorfully painted pots with Navajo designs. He has made very few vessels, but they belong in important collections of contemporary folk art.

Betty Manygoats has been exhibited at museums throughout the Southwest. Recently, her work was featured in a traveling exhibition that originated at the Museum of American Folk Art in New York City.

Christine McHorse

Quite simply put, Christine (Chris) McHorse of Santa Fe is New Mexico's best-known Navajo potter. Her unique vision developed out of the melding of three cultures—Navajo, Pueblo, and Anglo. Her work has earned her numerous awards and ribbons and garnered respect throughout the art world for the proud tradition of Navajo pottery.

"I am a hundred percent Navajo," she proudly proclaims, "but most of my life has been spent outside of the reservation. I was born on December 21, 1948, and raised in the Morenci-Clifton area of southeastern Arizona, where my father, Mark Nofchissey, worked in the copper mines. My summers were spent herding sheep with my grandmother in Croff Canyon [near Ganado]. In summer, I would live in Grandmother's hogan and learn the Navajo Way."

In 1966, McHorse graduated from The Institute of American Indian Arts in Santa Fe (a high school that offers some college-level courses) and then took a year of post-graduate work there. Three years after graduation from high school, she married Joel McHorse, a Pueblo Indian from Taos whose Texas cowboy father was Irish. Joel McHorse is a well-regarded silversmith, and their two sons, Joel Jr. and Jonathan, are becoming smiths in their own right.

Christine McHorse acquired her basic pottery skills from her husband's family in Taos. "Joel's grandmother, Lena Archuleta, taught me how to make the traditional pottery of the Taos Pueblo. Lena ran a curio shop [inside the charming old adobe Taos Pueblo] and worked with micaceous clay," McHorse relates. The traditional Taos pot is a simple, elegant vessel made from the area's readily available micaceous clay. It has thin walls that contain flecks of glistening mica and very few decorative elements. A Taos pot may be used for water storage, though it is slightly porous, and for cooking after it is fired. Taos pottery is otherwise fairly nondistinctive and not widely collected.

"Micaceous clay has some advantages over the typical gray Navajo clay which is found at Black Mesa," McHorse states. "It is readily available in the hills above Taos, and the flecks of metal temper the finished product—making the walls stronger. All clay

Christine McHorse, *Lizard Pot*, c. 1990. Pit-fired micaceous clay and piñon pitch, 5 1/2" height x 40" circumference.

135

must be screened to remove bits of stone and twigs; I screen mine twice so that the finished pot will not contain impurities."

Christine and Joel McHorse moved to Santa Fe about twelve years ago. They are presently building a home and plan to enlarge Christine McHorse's studio. Her mature artistry really developed after this move. "If you make a pot," she says, "You make it the best you can. My trade is now almost automatic. I have to touch every square inch of clay that goes into a pot and know that I put the clay there. Every piece must be better than the last. I feel that I am not bound by Navajo taboo or the demands of the Anglo art/pottery marketplace in Santa Fe. I am free to set my own standards."

McHorse has succumbed to the Anglo practice of kiln firing to some extent though she uses three distinct methods: (1) The pure Navajo style in an open pit; (2) The Anglo method in an electric kiln; and (3) A hybrid system firing first in a kiln and then outdoors. "I have discovered," she explained, "that the accidental interaction of fire clouds and piñon pitch are natural ingredients and essential elements for some of my work. Fire clouds do not appear in kiln-fired ware, and piñon pitch is not necessary to make it watertight. If a work is fired in a kiln and then refired in a pit, I can control the clouds to some extent, and the vessel will have the toughness of one that is fired in a kiln. In the end, it all depends on the result I want to achieve."

Opposite: Christine McHorse, *Crow Pot,* 1991. Kiln-fired and pit-fired micaceous clay, piñon pitch, and beeweed, 16 1/2" height x 39" circumference.

Many dealers and collectors prefer McHorse pots that are fired solely in a kiln. In these vessels, the artist explores the beauty and purity of form and the endless possibilities that can be achieved from micaceous clay. We prefer the pottery in which she uses elements of Navajo design and legend—which reveres the almost religious depth of spirit that comes out of the accidental interaction of earth, piñon pitch, and fire.

Christine McHorse has a resume that lists four pages of exhibitions, honors, and awards in this country, Germany, and Canada. For instance, McHorse has won a ribbon at Santa Fe's prestigious Indian Market every year that she entered the judging since her initial admission in 1984. In 1992, a justifiably confident McHorse came to "market" with only two pots—both won blue ribbons in different categories. There was a line of would-be purchasers waiting at her booth when she returned from the judging; McHorse went home by mid-morning—sold out. According to McHorse, "The ribbons and things are just bonuses. What I like is the opportunity to work without restraint."

Linda Nez

When the dark gray shadows of sunrise and the blue-red light of early evening make their way into Tanner Wash beneath Echo Cliffs, Linda Nez will be sitting in front of her loom, with a handmade comb in her left hand and yarn in her right hand. "It's an eight-hour-a-day job," she says. "The only job I have."

Weaving pictorial rugs was a career of choice for Linda Nez—one that she sought out. "I found myself with five years of schooling and in need of a job," she remembers. It isn't easy work, sitting in the tortuous position preferred by Navajo women—hands flying over warp and woof. "When I was young [about 14 years of age]," she explains, "I wanted to learn. My mother [Francis Sampson] was making rugs, but she wouldn't teach me. Mother said that she needed me to take care of the sheep and goats so she'd have the time to work on her own rugs."

Opposite: Linda Nez, *Carnival,* 1992.
Pictorial rug, commercial yarn,
30 ¹/₂" x 57".

Nez made her own loom and began working independently. "I knew from the beginning that I wanted to make pictorials. My first rug was a small scene of Grand Canyon," she says. "It took me four or five months to complete." Linda Nez doesn't want her age revealed, but she agreed to allow us to say that she is in her mid-thirties, and she has three girls and two boys.

The building of the Glen Canyon Dam and the creation of Lake Powell has brought tourism and industry to the area, but the resulting prosperity has meant very little to the residents of The Gap and Bitter Springs. There are many Navajo women weaving in the area. "My aunt, Susie Black, was probably the first to make pictures, but she is dead now," Nez says. "She made birds and butterflies. My mother lives over there in that green trailer [pointing north] and still makes rugs, but most are not pictorials. Sara Tso, who can make about anything, lives high up the ridge, and I am related by marriage to Florence Riggs over in Tuba City, but nobody can make them like me. The colors are in my head. I like to make pictures to really bring out the colors. I sketch out my own pictures [on the warp of the loom with magic marker], and then I fill them in with the colors right out of my head. And I don't care what a trader may want. I make my own pictures and if one trader won't buy it—I'll find another who will."

Innovative pictorials are hard to sell. The traders aren't looking for them and most do not like bright and unusual colors. A good-sized pictorial may take more than four

months to make; the unusual designs, even curved lines (faces, for instance) require very detailed work. Since pictorials are more difficult to weave than standard patterns, a weaver with the skill of a Linda Nez demands high prices. Many traders at smaller posts like The Gap cannot afford to pay these prices. But others, like Glenn and Gregg Leighton at the Notah Dineh (Ute-Navajo) post at Cortez, Colorado; Bill Malone at the Hubbell Trading Post; Mary Jones at Chinle's Thunderbird Lodge; and Bill Foutz at Foutz's Shiprock Trading Post, carry the very best in contemporary pictorial weaving. Gregg Leighton, who is a rug expert and judge, told us: "I won't quibble with a weaver like Linda Nez; what she asks is what I'll pay. I only wish she could make more rugs."

The rug she was working on during the day of our visit was a large, unique pictorial depicting Navajo using a traditional sweat house. It included nude men and women in a typical Navajo landscape. When we asked her about inspiration for the carnival scene we had recently purchased, she replied: "I once saw a traveling carnival from a car window as I drove by in Kayenta (near Monument Valley). The colors really stuck in my mind. This year I hear that a carnival is coming to Tuba City; I hope I can go."

There is often confusion over the name of the maker of a particular rug. Family members sometimes bring in rugs that may have been woven by an aunt or uncle, for instance. The trader honestly may not be able to determine who made the rug, but sometimes a trader or, as often happens, a subsequent owner will upgrade a rug deliberately, replacing the name of the actual weaver with one that is better known. Linda Nez is proud of her work and aware of this practice. Therefore, on recent rugs, she has sewn her initials (L.N.) into the lower right hand corner of the rug. This may be the beginning of a new Navajo practice. Historically, rugs have not been signed by the maker.

Revolutionary changes in weaving are on their way in remote areas of the Navajo homeland—watch for them.

Florence Riggs

Florence Riggs learned her craft from two generations of fine Navajo weavers. Her grandmother, Laura Nez, is still working in Tuba City—weaving traditional patterns. Louise Nez,
her mother, lives in a trailer in Farmington. Recently, under the influence of her daughter,
Louise Nez has switched from the storm patterns of her youth to pictorials.

But Florence Riggs is the star pictorialist of the family. She was born in 1962, in
Beryl, Utah, where her family was temporarily working, picking potatoes. Her mother

herded sheep in the Tuba City area, and Florence grew up
there. "The sheep are gone now—sold," Riggs explains. "After
I graduated from Tuba City High School, I worked at Bashas'
(an Arizona-based supermarket), Thriftway, and at Van's Trading
Company in Tuba City. When I got married to Perry [a diesel
mechanic in Tuba City, where the couple currently lives] and the
children started to come, I decided that babysitters were too
expensive and began to weave for a living, like my mother and
grandmother before me. I believe that every weaver should start on
traditional patterns, as I did. Traditionals are easier. The lines are
straight or slanted [not curved], and you can just copy what it is the trader wants.
Today, I will still do traditionals on order, but what I really want to make is pictures
that have never been done before."

In early October of 1992, we visited Florence Riggs at the home of her mother,
Louise Nez, in Farmington. Mother and daughter were working in the cramped-
for-space living room on a type of loom that we had never seen before—a double
loom. "My brother [Bill Nez] designed and built this loom for us," Florence Riggs
says. "It gives me the chance to visit with mother, and both of us can weave our
own rugs at the same time."

The two rugs the women were weaving on the large, steel-framed double loom
illustrate recent developments in the art of pictorial weaving. Louise Nez's rug was a
colorful farm scene, right out of her early life tending sheep. Florence Riggs, on the
other hand, was working on a present-day detailed representation of Foutz's Shiprock
Trading Post. To some, the picture may appear to be idealistic, and there are elements
of romance in it, but the details are of the post as it looks today, down to the items
on the shelves and the bald head of the trader (Bill Foutz).

141

Above: Florence Riggs, *Bill Foutz (with Bald Head), Shiprock Trading Post*, 1992. Pictorial rug, commercial yarn, 31" x 48".
Opposite: Florence Riggs, *Circus Scene*, 1992. Pictorial rug, commercial yarn, 31" x 48".

Florence Riggs gets her ideas from her imagination, as well as from magazines like Southwest Art and New Mexico. "After I get an idea," she explains, "I ask my brother [Bill Nez] to draw it out for me in outline." Bill Nez sketches a cartoonlike drawing of the original idea on used corrugated cardboard with a magic marker. Riggs then transfers the drawing and enlarges it, filling in details from her memory as she goes along. She draws freehand with black magic marker directly on the warp of the loom.

Riggs keeps a cardboard box filled with skeins of brightly colored wool at the ready near her loom. She buys the wool at the Navajo cooperative in Tuba City and at various trading posts. "The colors," she says, "come to me as I go along. I use colors that seem right. Bill Foutz likes bright colors but he doesn't like yellow. Too bad! I do!"

One of Florence Riggs' recent rugs, in fact, features a circus ring master basking in the beam of a yellow spotlight. "I've never seen a circus," Riggs said, "but I'd sure like to if one comes to Farmington or Tuba City."

Ida Sahmie

"My Grandmother, Irene Yazzie, warned me: 'Paint sacred Yei figures—burn them in fire—and you'll go blind, Ida,'" Sahmie painfully relates. "I fear that her prediction is coming true." That's the situation she described to us in a frantic telephone call from Albuquerque, where, in 1990, she was taking a computer course at the International Business College. "I can't read the computer screen good, and I won't wear glasses. I need a Blessingway ceremony, but I can't afford the medicine man's fee." This conversation illustrates the personal dilemma of a twentieth-century Navajo woman trying to cope with the ghosts of tradition.

Opposite: Ida Sahmie, *Pot with Yei Figures,* 1990. Fired clay, slip, and bee-weed, 8 1/4" height x 39" circumference.

Despite Grandmother Yazzie's warning, Ida Sahmie makes exquisite pottery, decorated with Yeibichai figures. Born in 1960, she grew up in a hogan in dirt-track country near Pine Springs, Arizona. In 1986, Ida Nobell, from a traditional Navajo family of weavers, did the almost unthinkable; she married Andrew ("Louie") Sahmie, who was not only a Hopi but a descendant of the great potter Nampeyo, who inspired the revival of Hopi pottery in the early years of the twentieth century. Her mother-in-law, Priscilla Namingha, is one of the most respected contemporary Hopi potters. The Navajos have been feuding with their Pueblo neighbors for more than a century, and there was a period of uneasiness. "But," says Sahmie, "we have worked it all out now."

Shortly after their marriage, the couple took up residence in a large trailer just south of the Hopi village of Polacca, Arizona, where she could easily observe Hopi ways. "In 1984, I remember watching my future mother-in-law make pottery," Sahmie remembers, "and I needed something to do with my hands, so that year, I began making pottery. My sisters-in-law (Hopi potters Rachel and Jean Sahmie) did not think it right for me to use Hopi designs, so I decorate with sacred pictures from my Navajo heritage."

Sahmie uses light-brown to creamy-yellow Hopi clay and fires with cedar in an open pit in back of her trailer. The pots are held over the fire on a grate and covered with cow chips. "Fire clouds," present in most Navajo pottery, do not appear in Hopi ware because the ash does not come in contact with the clay. Her vessels are so delicate and the walls so thin that many are lost in firing. Sahmie decorates with various clay slips she digs herself from secret places. Her slips range from brown to red and white

144

to black. She also uses beeweed, a form of wild spinach, which is first boiled down and then turns black in the firing process. The Yei designs and the other decorative elements are painted onto the unfired clay with yucca needles and thin brushes that allow her to make extremely delicate and graceful lines.

On some Sahmie vessels, the Yei dance at night by firelight. She is, we believe, the only potter to add the realism and mystery of darkness to depictions of ceremonial scenes..

The Sahmies live a short distance west of the Keams Canyon Trading Post, and she was discovered by Bruce McGee. Her work is always available in the extensive gallery at the post, Keams Canyon Arts and Crafts. Sahmie has been exhibited at most major museums in the Southwest and is generally featured wherever fine Indian pottery is sold.

Ida Sahmie, *Yeibichai Dance, Cut-Out Design,* 1989.
Fired clay, slip, and beeweed,
8 1/4" height x 39" circumference.

146

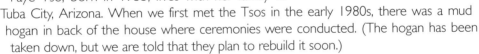

Faye Tso

Faye Tso is an unlikely revolutionary; she dresses in traditional velvet accented with turquoise jewelry, wears her hair in the traditional Navajo bun, and speaks very little English. She is a practicing Navajo herbalist married to a medicine man (and the mother of another) who has raised eight children (four sons and four daughters). All follow the Navajo Way. But Faye Tso is also one of the most innovative of the elder generation of Navajo potters.

Emmett Tso, her medicineman husband, does not find any contradiction in Faye Tso's achievement in helping to vitalize Navajo art. "Pottery is used in Navajo ceremonies," he explains. "Fire, cloud, and earth are all part of the Navajo Way. And Faye, my son Irving, and I are medicine men [when we first met Irving Tso, he was the youngest Navajo medicine man[5]] and know how to properly treat the subject matter; we can depict Yei figures, etc., without bad ramifications, just as Hastiin Klah did before us."[6] For additional protection, the Tsos have had ceremonies performed to protect them from harm, and so far pottery-making has brought them only good fortune.

Faye Tso, born in 1933, lives with her family in Tuba City, Arizona. When we first met the Tsos in the early 1980s, there was a mud hogan in back of the house where ceremonies were conducted. (The hogan has been taken down, but we are told that they plan to rebuild it soon.)

After Tso had completed only two years of school, her mother died and she had to leave school to help care for two sisters. The Tsos herd sheep and goats on land that they claim, but a portion of their claim is evidently disputed by the Hopis. In the 1980s, when we visited Faye Tso, she explained that gunfire had been exchanged that day because Hopis had encroached on her property.

Tso learned pottery making from "old, old Grandmother," probably a relative of her husband's. Then, in the 1970s, she worked with Rose Williams, Emmett's aunt and the doyenne of Shonto Corners, mastering the basic techniques that are common to all Navajo pottery makers. At first, she made utilitarian ware—casseroles, pitchers, and plates. But even this early work was distinguished in that it was decorated with

147

appliquéd ears of corn and Yeibichai figures—unlike the other plain ware that was being made at the time.

In the 1980s, when the demand for utilitarian pottery had dried up, Tso made the quantum jump into art pottery. "It was in the middle of the decade," says Bruce McGee, the trader at Keams Canyon, "that Faye began to bring in large vessels decorated with Yeibichai and Corn Maiden figures which were totally unlike anything we had seen before."

In the mid-1980s, Tso made a traditional drum pot with a biyo' in the form of a squash blossom necklace, turned it upside down, and pulled the face of her husband out of the wet clay. This portrait of Emmett was truly revolutionary. The Navajo have made numerous animals, playtoys for children, and decorative figurines out of clay, but this was the first-known serious portrait. "I tried to persuade her to do others," said Bruce McGee, "and she has sculpted—warriors and medicine men—but the inverted drum pot portrait of her husband remains unique."

Tso has experimented with various slips of clay and has used the dung of sheep, goats, and cattle during the firing process to change the color of the clay from golden orange to almost black. At one point, her son Irving, who was taking art classes in high school, persuaded her to use commercial clay provided by the Tuba City High School and to fire in their electric kiln. We do not believe that the resulting kiln-fired works have the depth of sensitivity of her other pots, but experimentation is essential to artistic growth.

Emmett Tso will, on occasion, break the taboo prohibiting men from working in clay. His pots are not as graceful as those of his wife, but they are, nevertheless, very interesting and his designs Navajo in origin. Faye Tso will not take the credit for teaching her husband how to pot, but she has been instrumental in instructing several other Navajos. Jimmy Wilson, Penny Emerson, her daughter Myra Tso Kaye and son Irving, as well as others have all benefited from her knowledge. One example of her advice was repeated by the well-known potter Penny Emerson. When she began to pot, Tso told her: "I'll be happy to teach you what I know, but if the clay doesn't like you, you will never be able to make a good pot."

Tso has demonstrated her art at the Museum of Northern Arizona in Flagstaff. She has participated in Santa Fe's Indian Market and was included in Folk Art of the People: Navajo Works at the Craft Alliance Gallery and Education Center, St. Louis, Missouri. A bust of a "Navajo Warrior" was in the *Cutting Edge* exhibition that recently toured the country under the sponsorship of the Museum of American Folk Art in New York City.

Faye Tso, Decorated *Bean Pot,*
Incised Corn Maiden Figures, 1987.
Fired clay and piñon pitch,
14" height x 31" circumference.

Notes to Western Region

1 Several of Klah's nieces (Gladys and Irene) assisted in the later weavings. The material concerning the Wheelwright's collection was provided by Susan Brown McGreevy, President of the Board of Directors of that museum. (Klah's first name is sometimes given as "Hosteen." We have used the Wheelwright's spelling, "Hastiin.")

2 Charlene Cerny, *Navajo Pictorial Weaving,* Exhibition Catalogue (Santa Fe, NM: Museum of New Mexico Foundation, 1975), 6. Estimates as to the number of contemporary Navajo weavers very greatly. It has been said there may be as many as twelve to twenty-eight thousand Navajo weavers today. Ann Lane Hedlund, *Reflections on the Weaver's World: The Gloria Ross Collection of Contemporary Navajo Weaving* (Denver: Denver Art Museum, 1992), 23. The problem of determining the number of weavers is complicated by the different ways of defining a weaver—one who knows how to weave, one who has made some rugs, one who weaves full-time, part-time, etc.

3 See Frank McNitt, *The Indian Traders* (Norman and London, University of Oklahoma Press, 1962), 273.

4 Traditionally, more rugs are made during hard times. In 1947, for example, when newspapers were reporting bad times among the Navajo, Mildred Carson Heflin who, with her husband Reuben, ran the Shonto Trading Post at the time, remarked that 1947 seemed no worse than usual "since few rugs were being brought in, and that was always a sign that no one was truly desperate."

5 See also James C. Faris, *The Nightway: A History and a History of Documentation of a Navajo Ceremonial* (Albuquerque: University of New Mexico Press, 1990), 98, listing Tso as the youngest of the contemporary Nightway medicine men.

6 See information on Hastiin Klah (page 118) who, together with Mary Cabot Wheelwright, founded the Wheelwright Museum of the American Indian.

Appendix A: The Artists

Johnson Antonio
Born April 15, 1931
Resides Lake Valley area, NM

Sheila Antonio
Born March 27, 1961
Resides Bisti area, NM

Elsie Benally
Birthdate unavailable
Resides Sweetwater, AZ

Sandy Beyale
Born December 20, 1971
Resides near Tsaya, NM

Delbert Buck
Born September 10, 1976
Resides Gallegos Wash (near
Farmington and Bloomfield), NM

Silas and Bertha Claw
Silas born December 15, 1913
Bertha born August 1926
Reside near Cow Springs and Shonto
Corner, AZ

Alice Cling
Born March 21, 1946
Resides near Shonto Corner, AZ

Matilda Damon
Born August 20, 1962
Resides Fruitland, NM

Mamie Deschillie
Born July 27, 1920
Resides Fruitland, NM

Louise Rose Goodman
Born December 25, 1937
Resides near Cow Springs, AZ

Ray Growler
Born April 4, 1965
Resides Shiprock, NM

Helen Greyeyes
Born April 15, 1938
Resides Tall Mountain, AZ

Bruce Hathale
Born October 23, 1956
Resides Tes Nez Iah, AZ

Dennis Hathale
Born June 6, 1961
Resides Farmington, NM

Roger Hathale
Born March 15, 1918
Resides Tes Nez Iah. AZ

Woody Herbert
Born c. 1926-1927
Resides Sweetwater, AZ

Dan Hot
Born July 10, 1932
Resides Sweetwater, AZ

Elizabeth Willeto Ignacio
Born July 11, 1926
Resides near Nageezi, NM

Lawrence Jacquaz
Born December 8, 1965
Resides Nageezi, NM

Edith Herbert John
Born April 7, 1961
Resides Sweetwater, AZ

Myra Tso Kaye
Born October 24, 1961
Resides Flagstaff, AZ

Ronald Malone
Born December 7, 1946
Resides Sweetwater, AZ

Betty Manygoats
Born January 30, 1945
Resides near Shonto Corner, AZ

Christine McHorse
Born December 21, 1948
Resides Santa Fe, NM

Linda Nez
Artist requested her age not be
revealed
Resides near Bitter Springs, AZ

Fannie Pete
Born February 10, 1958
Resides Gallegos Canyon (near
Bloomfield), NM

Julia Pete
Born April 1, 1974

Resides Gallegos Canyon (near
Bloomfield), NM

Dennis Pioche
Born November 25, 1965
Resides Aztec, NM

Florence Riggs
Born November 4, 1962
Resides Tuba City, AZ

Ida Sahmie
Born May 27, 1960
Resides Keams Canyon, AZ

Andrew Tsihnahjinnie
Born February 14 or November 14,
1916 (birth date of 1908 or 1909
also given)
Resides Rough Rock and Phoenix,
AZ

Faye Tso
Born 1933
Resides Tuba City, AZ

Charlie Willeto
Born February 20, 1897 or 1906
Died December 14, 1964
Resided near Nageezi, NM

Harold Willeto
Born December 2, 1959
Resides near Nageezi, NM

Leonard Willeto
Born May 20, 1955
Died August 2, 1984
Resided near Nageezi, NM

Robin Willeto
Born October 24, 1962
Resides near Nageezi, NM

Lorraine Williams
Born November 1, 1955
Resides Cortez, CO

Tom Yazzie
Born July 25, 1930
Resides Fort Defiance, AZ

Wilford and Lulu Yazzie
Wilford born August 16, 1946
Lulu born November 15, 1959
Reside in Sweetwater, AZ

Mamie Deschillie, one of the "superstars" of Navajo folk art, with two of her cutouts.

Appendix B: Navajo Origin Legend

There are various versions of the Navajo Creation Story (*Diné Bahane'*). The following is a summary based on Rough Rock Press's *Navajo History*, written by the Navajo for Navajo people and illustrated by one of the folk artists in this book, Andrew Tsihnahjinnie. For a more detailed version, see Paul G. Zolbrod, *Diné Bahane', The Navajo Creation Story* (Albuquerque: University of New Mexico Press, 1984).

BLACK WORLD—At the beginning was the Black World where only Spirit People and Holy People lived. This world, small in size, had four corners over which four cloud columns appeared. Where the black cloud and white cloud met in the east, First Man was formed. Where the yellow cloud and the blue cloud came together in the west, First Woman was formed. With her came an ear of yellow corn, white shell, and turquoise. Many kinds of insect beings also lived in the Black World. When the various beings fought among themselves, the population emerged upwards into the Blue World.

BLUE WORLD—When the beings climbed into the Blue World, they found many other beings living there, including bluebirds and other blue-feathered beings. In the second world, there were a number of chambers and the beings were at war with one another. First Man killed some of the warring animals, later restoring them to life. Because of the sorrow and suffering present in the Blue World, First Man and the others prepared to leave. First Man made a wand of jet, turquoise, abalone, and white shell, placing four footprints on the wand so the beings could stand on them and be carried up into the next world.

YELLOW WORLD—Bluebird was the first to reach the Third World. Next came First Man, First Woman, Coyote, and one of the insects, then the others. In the Yellow World, there was no sun. There came a great flood. First Man planted a female reed, which grew to the top of the sky. The people escaped by climbing up the reed into the Fourth World.

GLITTERING WORLD—Locust was the first being to come into the Fourth World. In this world, First Man and First Woman formed the four main sacred mountains from soil the First Man had gathered from mountains in the Third World. In this world, they made the first fire and a hogan out of logs, with the doorway facing east. The people wanted stronger light. First Man, First Woman, and Coyote placed stars in the sky. Next, First Man and First Woman made the sun and the moon, placing them in the sky. They then divided the year into four seasons.

First Man brought forth white corn; First Woman brought yellow corn. Turkey danced back and forth, and out of his feather coat dropped four kernels of corn. Next, Big Snake came forward, giving four seeds: the pumpkin, the watermelon, the cantaloupe, and the muskmelon. The harvest from these seeds was very large.

After the harvest, Turquoise Boy visited and slept with First Woman. First Man returned home and was very hurt. This was the first adultery. Subsequently, Yellow Fox, Blue Fox, and Badger sought out other women. First Man called the leaders and other men together to decide what should be done. The males decided to separate themselves from the women; they built a raft, crossing to the other side of the river with great difficulty (leaving the guilty men behind).

At first, the women did not mind being alone. In a few years, however, they became lazy and did not take care of their small field, which grew only weeds. The women became very hungry and called the men to come back. The leaders held a council and decided to take the women back. Cleansing ceremonies were held. After the proper ritual and sweat baths, both sexes were purified and returned to live with each other.

First Man and First Woman lived near Huerfano Mountain (*Dził Ná'ooditii*). These were the first beings to appear like the people known as humans. Crops were good, but there were monsters who killed and caused great concern. One morning at dawn, a baby girl came from within a cloud; this was Changing Woman. In time she grew up and had twin boys.

One of the twins, the older and braver, was known as Monster Slayer. His younger brother was Child Born of Water. Both boys had dreams and visions.

One day, they climbed into a hole in the ground, where they came face to face with Spider Woman. They asked for help in finding their father so he could kill the monsters. She promised to help, telling the Twins their father was the Sun. Spider Woman, warning the boys of the many hazards they would meet on their way to the Sun's house, taught them things only she knew. After overcoming many difficulties, they reached their destination, where the Twins were subjected to further tests by the Sun. Finally, after recognizing that the Twins were truly his sons, the Sun gave them weapons—the older, Lightning that Strikes Crooked, and the younger, Lightning that Flashes Straight. Monster Slayer and Child Born of Water then returned to Earth.

With the help of their new weapons, Monster Slayer and Child Born of Water killed the terrible and destructive monsters in their homeland. After climbing the four sacred mountains and seeing no more monsters, the Twins decided to visit the home of their father once again. The Sun gave the boys many gifts of corn, pollen, animals, and plants, requiring in return that he be allowed to destroy those who lived in houses.

Before the Sun began his destruction, however, the Holy People picked up a man and woman and pairs of all animals. A flood covered the earth. Finally, the waters went down, and the Holy People put back those they had saved.

After that, Monster Slayer became very tired; he lacked peace and harmony. One day, he was found almost beaten to death. The people held a meeting to decide how to help Monster Slayer. It is from this incident that the first Squaw Dance came. The ceremony was performed, and Monster Slayer recovered.

At the request of the Sun, Changing Woman and some of the people moved to the west. They became lonely, so she created more people (the first four clans). With their animals, the four groups later left for the east, accompanied by Talking God and Second Talking God. Additional legends describe the journey. At one point, the people grew tired and started to turn back. Changing Woman disapproved and instructed Talking God of the White Shell People and Talking God of the Turquoise People to have a Blessing Way Ceremony at specified places. This was done so the people would not turn back again.

The Holy People were close to the Navajos. Through their teachings, the power and beauty of the Holy People became known to the Navajos, and they increased and prospered.

Many more clans came into existence, and the small handful of people who had come into the Fourth World grew and grew until now one can speak with pride of the Navajo Nation.

Many of the people started moving from place to place. The home of the People eventually existed within the boundaries of the four sacred mountains (Mountain of the East, Mountain of the West, Mountain of the North, and Mountain of the South). One God was left within each of these mountains; that is why they are sacred. Eight other mountains also are holy.

There is a God (Yé'ii) whose body starts at the foot of Mount Taylor and curves all the way around the outside of the four sacred mountains with the head stopping at Blanca Peak. This was done to protect the People. The Navajos believe that if they spread out beyond that boundary, they may run into difficulties with nature and be out of harmony with the plan of the Gods.

GLOSSARY

Anasazi—"Ancient ones." This is the Navajo term for the Pueblo people who lived in the region from the fifth century until about 1300 A.D., at which time they mysteriously disappeared, perhaps because of several periods of severe drought and crop failure. (The reason for the disappearance of the Anasazi is still under study.) Ruins may be seen at such locations as Chaco Culture National Historic Park and Bandelier National Monument in New Mexico, and Arizona's Canyon de Chelly National Monument.

Appliqué—Decoration created by attaching modeled clay forms to the surface of vessels or figures. This method, long common in Pueblo ceramics, was also used by Navajo potters. Only recently, however, has it become a favored Navajo decorative technique.

Beeweed—Wild spinach plant boiled to juice by potters; it produces a black color when fired.

Biyo'—Traditional appliqué necklace just below the rim of a pot. A small break in the biyo', called atiin, or "the way out," is similar to the spirit line in weavings and the break in baskets, offering a path of escape for the energy and spirit put into creating the pot.

Brush Arbor—An open-sided structure, often constructed out of cedar poles, with a roof thatched with brush, such as oak branches. The arbor is used in summer for cooking and sometimes for sleeping in hot weather.

Census Form—Now called Tribal Enrollment Form. This form is issued to tribal members. In order to enroll, a person must be able to show that he or she is at least twenty-five percent Navajo.

Chapter Houses—In 1955, the Navajo Tribal Council recognized that the chapter system had long met a community need. In the late 1950s, the Tribe financed the building of chapter houses to serve as a forum for community issues, problems, grievances, and development. About a hundred chapter houses exist today, serving as general community centers.

Checkerboard Region—Portions of the reservation, such as the area around Carson's Trading Post, south of Farmington, are made up of a complex pattern of land holdings—railroad land and Executive Order Indian lands. Such areas have become known as the Checkerboard region, due to the different holdings.

Churro Sheep—A small, hardy breed of sheep introduced into the Southwest by the Spaniards in the late 1500s. The wool of the churro is ideal for weaving. While there has been crossbreeding, some strains could not survive on the reservation, and the wool of others, like the rambouillet crossbreeds, did not prove suitable for Navajo weaving.

Code Talkers—Because of the complexity of the Navajo language, largely unwritten at the beginning of World War II, it provided an excellent means of sending messages. Navajo "code talkers" served throughout the Pacific campaign, and, to a lesser extent, in Europe and Sicily; the enemy was never able to break the "code."

Coiling—The traditional method of Native American pottery-making in the Southwest. The Navajo method of coiling is distinctive in that the shaping of a vessel takes place as the piece is built rather than later. Also, the thinning and heightening of the walls is accomplished by pinching rather than scraping or paddling.

Diné—The People. Name used by the Navajo to refer to themselves. (Man, person, Navajo). The word is sometimes spelled Dineh or Dine'é.

Dinétah—Navajo homeland in the states of Arizona, New Mexico, and Utah. Also used as a reference to the "old Navajo country," a region in northern New Mexico occupied by the Navajo at the time of the advent of the Spaniards.

Dleesh—White clay used by the Navajos to paint their bodies during ceremonies. Several Navajo folk artists (like Johnson Antonio) have used dleesh as paint, particularly in their early works.

Fire Clouds—Black or blackish gray discolorations on the surface of a pot caused when ash comes in contact with the clay during firing. While many Pueblo potters try to avoid fire clouds, these clouds seldom bother the Navajo. Such clouds are one proof of traditional (rather than kiln) firing.

Folk Art—Work by untrained, self-taught artists. Sometimes called visionary, isolate, naive, or outsider art. The work is highly personal, idiosyncratic, nonutilitarian, representing an individual vision. The craft may be derived from communal traditions, but, as used here, something personal, innovative, must be added to qualify it as art. The craft may be learned, but the art is self-taught.

Hataałii—Medicine man, singer, chanter.

Handspun Yarn—Sometimes called homespun. Yarn produced by hand from raw wool, usually spun on a spindle or spinning wheel.

Hogan (or *hooghan*)—Home. A traditional Navajo dwelling, constructed with available material, such as timbers or stone, and covered or chinked with mud or cedar bark. The hogan is usually approximately circular, with one door facing east and a smoke hole or chimney in the center of the roof. The number of sides may vary, but the structure is frequently six- or eight-sided. While hogans are still common in the Navajo Nation, they may be used today for ceremonial purposes or storage rather than as a principal dwelling.

Incising—Scratching the surface of pottery with a sharp instrument while the clay is still damp, to produce decoration.

Land Dispute—A land dispute between the Navajos and the Hopis has been ongoing for more than a hundred years. The disputed land was partitioned under legislation enacted in 1974, but final settlement has not been reached. Officials of both tribes reached tentative agreement in 1992. However, objections have been raised, and the outcome is uncertain.

Loom—A handmade, upright, rectangular frame that supports the warps of a weaving. Originally, two posts were set in the ground, and two cross-pieces or braces were lashed to the posts. The distance between the posts in early looms was the length of a blanket.

Memory Aids—Drawings by medicine men, used to assist them in remembering particular ceremonies or chants. In some instances, these may be actual small sketches or partial sketches of sandpaintings.

Micaceous Clay—Clay containing mica flakes that produces pottery with a glittery surface. The clay is commonly used by Taos and Picuris potters, but very rarely by Navajos.

Native American Church—A religious movement with membership drawn from many tribes. It emphasizes the unity of Indians and involves eating the peyote cactus. In recent years, many Navajo have become members of the Church.

Navajo Kachinas—Occasionally, the Navajos make kachina dolls in imitation of their Hopi neighbors. Reputable dealers will label them as Navajo-made. Because these carvings are imitative rather than innovative, the makers have not been included in *The People Speak: Navajo Folk Art.*

Navajo Nation—In 1969, the "Navajo Nation" became the official designation for the Navajo tribe. Earlier, in 1924, Congress had declared all American Indians U. S. citizens, and in 1946, the Indian Claims Act was passed, allowing claims against the United States for lands taken in the westward expansion.

Navajo Way—The ordained and orderly way of life on earth. The Navajos believe that the universe is an orderly, all-inclusive unity of interrelated elements. Harmony is central to the Navajo Way. The condition desired is *hózhǫ́* or *hoozhǫǫh*—beautiful, harmonious, peaceful—integration of all forces into a harmonious world.

Pictorial Rugs—Nongeometric rugs incorporating recognizable images. There are a few early examples of pictorial Navajo rugs, but they did not become widespread until almost the end of the nineteenth century after the establishment of trading posts on the reservation and the advent of railroads in the Southwest. (Trains were a popular early subject.) Today, the subject matter is as varied as the artist's imagination. Statistically, however, pictorials represent a very small percentage of Navajo textiles. They are probably the earliest form of Navajo folk art. In general, the rugs are intended as wall hangings rather than for floor use.

Picker—As used here, a picker is an intermediary, one who purchases art from the maker or a remote trading post and resells it to a gallery or dealer in a large city.

Powwow—A meeting of Native Americans. Originally defined as a name for ceremonies and councils, it has come to mean any gathering or get-together of Native Americans for such purposes as dance demonstrations and socializing.

Sandpaintings—Also called drypaintings. As an essential part of Navajo ceremonies and curing rituals, strictly prescribed stylized designs are drawn on the ground, by a singer or under his direction, with colored sand, earth, and ground pigments, which include sandstones, mudstones, charcoal from oak, cornmeal, powdered flower petals, and plant pollens. Natural-colored sand (tan) is first placed on the floor as a base. The paintings vary in size, but 6' by 6', a size that will fit on the floor of an average hogan, is typical. At the end of the ritual, the sandpaintings are destroyed. Because of the supernatural power of sandpaintings, they were seldom reproduced outside of a ceremonial setting until the 1950s. (There were some exceptions. A few scholars and traders had reproductions made. Franc Newcomb, a friend of Hostiin Klah, recorded over seven hundred sandpaintings. And Klah himself, a medicine man and co-founder of the Wheelwright Museum, recorded sandpaintings and wove a number of sandpainting rugs to ensure that vital tribal knowledge was preserved. Klah believed his powers protected him from harm that would otherwise befall one who made sandpaintings outside of the proper ceremonial setting.) Since the 1970s, sandpaintings have developed as an art form. Not all Navajos, however, approve, and the artists and weavers are generally careful to avoid exact reproduction of sacred sandpaintings. By intentionally changing at least one element in the design, color symbolism, or composition, Navajo artists believe that the Holy People will not be called and that the paintings will therefore remain secular objects.

Sweathouse—Small hut where a bather pours water on hot stones until dirt and perspiration can be rubbed off. Sweathouses are also the site of various rituals and cleansing ceremonies, dating back to the Navajo Origin Legend.

Taboo *(Bahádzid)*—Something feared or injurious. The word is applied to anything that should be avoided or dreaded as contrary to good tradition.

Temper—Any coarse material added to clay to facilitate workability and drying. The Navajos use pottery sherds, sand, and volcanic rock.

Trade Blanket—Commercially created, machine-woven blanket for an American Indian market, meant for wearing. These blankets are usually in the form of fringed shawls for women and bound robes for men. The trade blankets have been worn by Indians since at least the 1860s and are still used today. The more important design elements, like the cross, the arrow, and the zigzag, trace their roots to Native American tradition. Among the best known and most popular are the blankets produced by the Pendleton Woolen Mills of Oregon. Pendleton is the only surviving company of all the major manufacturers of American Indian trade blankets in the early 1900s.

Trading Post *(Naalyéhé bá hooghan)*—"A house with things of value." The early trading posts were small general stores, licensed by the government, that sprang up on the reservation after the Navajos returned from Bosque Redondo in 1868. These posts played a major role in the economic life of the Navajo during the late 1800s and early 1900s. During this period, traders lived on the post and were members of the community. Among the most popular items were staples such as flour, coffee, potatoes, bacon, sugar, canned tomatoes and peaches, salt, and baking powder. Household equipment, knives, saddles, and bridles could also be purchased at the posts. In trade, the Navajos supplied lambs, wool, kids, piñon nuts, and rugs. The traders generally accepted pawn and also provided credit to their customers. Storekeepers often wrote letters for the Navajos and performed other services such as dispensing medicine or interceding in quarrels. The posts also served a social function. In the early days, the traders and their families constituted, for all practical purposes, the white world. By about 1890, the traders began to realize the importance of Navajo weaving. They sent for yarn from Germantown, Pennsylvania; they found eastern markets for rugs. By the early 1900s, the rug market was booming. In the process, however, the traders felt obliged to produce designs popular in the East. Thus, it was that traders like J. B. Moore at Crystal and J. Lorenzo Hubbell at Ganado developed designs for the weavers, resulting in a tendency toward standardization of patterns. Following World War II, the importance of the trading post declined, as other stores opened near the reservation and automobiles made travel more convenient. Many of the posts either closed or were purchased by a convenience chain such as Thriftway. Only a few, such as the Shonto Trading Post and Keams Canyon, are still general stores (carrying clothing, etc.), serving as trading posts in the traditional sense.

Warp—Parallel yarns strung on a loom. Weft yarns are woven over and under the warps.

Wedding Vase—Double-spouted vase, a popular form that appears in Native American pottery, including Navajo pottery.

Weft—Yarns woven over and under warp yarns, which are attached to the loom.

Yeibichai (also *Yé'ii Bicheii* or *Ye-Be-Chai*)—Sacred Navajo winter healing ceremonial or Nightway Chant, lasting nine nights. (It may take place only after the first frost when snakes are in hibernation and there is no danger from lightning.) Literally, the term means "grandfather of the Yé'ii and leader of the Yé'ii impersonators (masked dancers)" in the ceremony. For additional information on the Navajo ceremonial and the Hataałii who perform it, see James C. Faris, *The Nightway.*

Yei or *Yé'ii*—A class of supernatural beings, Holy People. The Yei are often depicted in Navajo pictorial rugs.

Yucca—A southwestern desert plant with long narrow leaves. Some Navajo potters use yuccas leaves as paint brushes.

BIBLIOGRAPHY

This selected bibliography lists the books and reference sources used in the preparation of this work as well as a number of books and publications that provide an overview of folk art in general.

NAVAJO ARTS AND NAVAJO FOLK ART

Amsden, Charles A. *Navaho Weaving: Its Technic and History*. Santa Ana, CA: Fine Arts Press, 1934. Reprint. Glorieta, NM: Rio Grande Press, 1990.

Bernstein, Bruce D., and Susan Brown McGreevy. *Anii Ánáá-daalyaa' Ígíí: Continuity & Innovation in Recent Navajo Art*. Exhibition Catalog. Santa Fe, NM: Wheelwright Museum of the American Indian, 1988.

Brugge, David M., H. Diane Wright, and Jan Bell. "Navajo Pottery." *Plateau Magazine* 58, no. 2, (1987).

Campbell, Tyrone, and Joel and Kate Kopp. *Navajo Pictorial Weaving 1880-1950*. New York: Penguin Books USA, Dutton Studio Books, 1991.

Cerny, Charlene. *Navajo Pictorial Weaving*. Santa Fe: The Museum of New Mexico Foundation, 1975.

Hartman, Russell P., and Jan Musial. *Navajo Pottery: Traditions and Innovations*. Flagstaff, AZ: Northland Press, 1987.

Hedlund, Ann Lane. *Reflections of the Weaver's World*. Denver: Denver Art Museum, 1992.

Kaufman, Alice, and Christopher Selser. *The Navajo Weaving Tradition: 1650 to the Present*. New York: E.P. Dutton, 1985.

Kent, Kate Peck. *Navajo Weaving: Three Centuries of Change*. Santa Fe: School of American Research Press, 1985.

La Chapelle, Greg. *Navajo Folk Sculpture: Alfred Walleto*. Santa Fe, NM: Wheelwright Museum of the American Indian, n.d.

Newcomb, Franc J., and Gladys A. Reichard. *Sandpaintings of the Navajo Shooting Chant*. New York: J.J. Augustin, [1937]; Mineola, NY: Dover Publications,1975.

Parezo, Nancy J. *Navajo Sandpainting: From Religious Act to Commercial Art*. Tucson: University of Arizona Press, 1983.

Reichard, Gladys A. *Navajo Medicine Man*. New York: J.J. Augustin, 1939. Reprint. *Navajo Medicine Man Sandpaintings*. New York: Dover Publications, 1977.

Roessel, Robert A., Jr. *Navajo Arts and Crafts*. Rough Rock, AZ: Navajo Curriculum Center, 1983.

Rosenak, Charles. "Carved in Cottonwood: Dolls Depict Life on the Bisti." In *Indians of New Mexico*, edited by Richard C. Sandoval and Ree Sheck. Santa Fe: New Mexico Magazine, 1990.

———. *Folk Art of the People: Navajo Works*. St. Louis: Craft Alliance Gallery and Education Center, 1987.

———. "Navajo Pottery: A New Twist on an Old Tradition." *The Clarion* 13, no. 3 (Summer 1988).

Schiffer, Nancy N. *Navajo Arts and Crafts*. West Chester, PA: Schiffer Publishing, 1991.

———. *Pictorial Weavings of the Navajo*. West Chester, PA: Schiffer Publishing, 1991.

Tschopik, Harry, Jr. *Navaho Pottery Making: An Inquiry into the Affinities of Navaho Painted Pottery*. Cambridge: Papers of the Peabody Museum of American Archaeology and Ethnology, Harvard University, 1941.

FOLK ART—GENERAL

Adele, Lynne. *Black History/Black Vision: The Visionary Image in Texas*. Exhibition Catalog. Austin: Archer M. Huntington Art Gallery, University of Texas, 1989.

Babcock, Barbara A., Guy Monthan, and Doris Monthan. *The Pueblo Storyteller: Development of a Figurative Ceramic Tradition*. Tucson: University of Arizona Press, 1986.

Baking in the Sun: Visionary Images from the South (Selections from the Collection of Sylvia and Warren Lowe). Exhibition Catalog. Lafayette: University Art Museum, University of Southwestern Louisiana, 1987.

Bishop, Robert. *American Folk Sculpture*. New York: E.P. Dutton, 1974.

———. *Folk Painters of America*. New York: E.P. Dutton, 1979.

Black Art—Ancestral Legacy: The African-Impulse in African-American Art. Exhibition Catalog. Dallas: Dallas Museum of Art, 1989.

Briggs, Charles L. *The Wood Carvers of Cordova, New Mexico: Social Dimensions of an Artistic "Revival."* Knoxville: University of Tennessee Press, 1980.

Burrison, John A. *Brothers in Clay: The Story of Georgia Folk Pottery*. Athens: University of Georgia Press, 1983.

Cahill, Holger. *Masters of Popular Painting*. New York: Museum of Modern Art, 1938.

Cahill, Holger, Maxmillien Gauthier, Jean Cassou, Dorothy C. Miller, et al. *Masters of Popular Painting: Modern Primitives of Europe and America*. New York: Museum of Modern Art, 1938.

Cardinal, Roger. *Outsider Art*. New York: Praeger Publishers, 1972.

Coe, Ralph T. *Lost and Found Traditions: Native American Art 1965-1985*. Seattle: University of Washington Press and American Federation of Arts, 1986.

Dillingham, Rick, with Melinda Elliott. *Acoma & Laguna Pottery*. Santa Fe: School of American Research Press, 1992.

Elijah Pierce Woodcarver. Exhibition catalog. Columbus, OH: Columbus Museum of Art, 1992.

Finster, Howard, as told to Tom Patterson. *Howard Finster, Stranger from Another World: Man of Visions Now on This Earth.* New York: Abbeville Press, 1989.

Frank, Larry. *New Kingdom of the Saints: Religious Art of New Mexico 1780-1907.* Santa Fe: Red Crane Books, 1992.

George, Phyllis. *Kentucky Crafts: Handmade and Heartfelt.* New York: Crown Publishers, 1989.

Goodrich, Lloyd. *What Is American in American Art.* New York: M. Knoedler and Co., 1979.

Hartigan, Lynda Roscoe. *Made with Passion: The Hemphill Folk Art Collection in the National Museum of American Art.* Exhibition Catalog. Washington: National Museum of American Art, Smithsonian Institution Press, 1990.

Hemphill, Herbert W., Jr., and Julia Weissman. *Twentieth-Century American Folk Art and Artists.* New York: E.P. Dutton, 1974.

Horwitz, Elinor Lander. *Contemporary American Folk Artists.* Philadelphia: J. B. Lippincott, 1975.

It'll Come True: Eleven Artists First and Last. Exhibition Catalog. Lafayette, LA: Artists' Alliance, 1992.

Jacka, Lois Essary, and Jerry Jacka. *Beyond Tradition: Contemporary Indian Art and Its Evolution.* Flagstaff, AZ: Northland Publishing Company, 1988.

Janis, Sidney. *They Taught Themselves: American Primitive Painters of the 20th Century.* New York: Dial Press, 1942.

Johnson, Jay, and William C. Ketchum, Jr. *American Folk Art of the Twentieth Century.* New York: Rizzoli, 1983.

Kapoun, Robert W., with Charles J. Lohrman. *Language of the Robe: American Indian Trade Blankets.* Salt Lake City: Peregrine Smith Books, 1992.

Kaufman, Barbara Wahl, and Didi Barrett. *A Time to Reap: Late Blooming Folk Artists.* Exhibition Catalog. South Orange, NJ: Seton Hall University and Museum of American Folk Art, 1985.

Lampell, Ramona, and Millard Lampell, with David Larkin. *O, Appalachia: Artists of the Southern Mountains.* New York: Stewart, Tabori & Chang, 1989.

Larson-Martin, Susan, and Lauri Robert Martin. *Pioneers in Paradise: Folk and Outsider Artists of the West Coast.* Exhibition Catalog. Long Beach, CA: Long Beach Museum of Art, 1984.

Lipman, Jean, and Tom Armstrong, eds. *American Folk Painters of Three Centuries.* New York: Hudson Hills Press and Whitney Museum of Art, 1980.

Livingston, Jane, and John Beardsley. *Black Folk Art in America, 1930-1980.* Jackson: University Press of Mississippi, 1982.

Maresca, Frank, and Roger Ricco. *American Self-Taught: Paintings and Drawings by Outsider Artists.* New York: Alfred A. Knopf, 1993.

Mariott, Alice. *Maria: The Potter of San Ildefonso.* Norman: University of Oklahoma Press, 1948.

Monthan, Guy, and Doris Monthan. *Nacimientos: Nativity Scenes by Southwest Indian Artisans.* Flagstaff, AZ: Northland Press, 1979.

Naives and Visionaries. Exhibition Catalog. New York: E. P. Dutton and Walker Art Center, 1974.

One Space/Three Visions. Exhibition Catalog. Albuquerque, NM: Albuquerque Museum, 1979.

Orr-Cahill, Christina. *Cat and a Ball on a Waterfall: 200 Years of California Folk Painting and Sculpture.* Exhibition Catalog. Oakland, CA: Oakland Museum Art Department, 1986.

Outsiders: An Art without Precedent or Tradition. Exhibition Catalog. London: Arts Council of Great Britain, 1979.

Rambling on My Mind: Black Folk Art of the Southwest. Exhibition Catalog. Dallas: Museum of African-American Life and Culture, 1987.

Rosenak, Chuck, and Jan Rosenak. *Museum of American Folk Art Encyclopedia of Twentieth-Century American Folk Art and Artists.* New York: Abbeville Press, 1990.

Sandoval, Richard C., and Ree Sheck, eds. *Indians of New Mexico.* Santa Fe: New Mexico Magazine, 1990.

Schuyt, Michael, Joost Elffers, and George R. Collins. *Fantastic Architecture: Personal and Eccentric Visions.* New York: Harry N. Abrams, 1980.

Spivey, Richard L. *Maria.* Flagstaff, AZ: Northland Publishing, 1979.

Thévoz, Michel. *Art Brut.* New York: Skira/Rizzoli, 1976.

Trimble, Stephen. *Talking with the Clay: The Art of Pueblo Pottery.* Santa Fe: School of American Research Press, 1987.

Tuchman, Maurice, and Carol S. Eliel. *Parallel Visions: Modern Artists and Outsider Art.* Exhibition Catalog. Los Angeles and Princeton: Los Angeles County Museum of Art and Princeton University Press, 1992.

Turner, J.F. *Howard Finster, Man of Visions: The Life and Work of a Self-Taught Artist.* New York: Alfred A. Knopf, 1989.

Wampler, Jan. *All Their Own: People and the Places They Build.* Cambridge, MA: Schenkman Publishing Company, 1977.

Whiteford, Andrew Hunter. *Southwestern Indian Baskets: Their History and Their Makers.* Santa Fe: School of American Research Press, 1988.

Zug, Charles G.,III. *Turners and Burners: The Folk Potters of North Carolina.* Chapel Hill: University of North Carolina Press, 1986.

NAVAJO REFERENCES—GENERAL

Aberle, David F. "Peyote Religion Among the Navajo." In *Southwest. Vol 10 of Handbook of North American Indians,* edited by Alfonso Ortiz. Washington: Smithsonian Institution, 1983.

Adams, William Y. "Shonto: A Study of the Role of the Trader in a Modern Navajo Community." Ph.D. Dissertation, University of Arizona, 1958 (UMI Dissertation Services).

Babbitt, James E., Martha Blue, Willow Roberts, and Joan Brundige-Baker. "Historic Trading Posts." *Plateau Magazine* 57, no. 3 (1986).

Bailey, Garrick, and Roberta Glenn Bailey. *A History of the Navajos: The Reservation Years.* Santa Fe: School of American Research Press, 1986.

Boyce, George A. *When Navajos Had Too Many Sheep: The 1940's.* San Francisco: Indian Historian Press, 1974.

Brugge, David M. Navajo Prehistory and History to 1850. In *Handbook of North American Indians*, Vol. 10, Southwest,ed. by Alfonso Ortiz. Washington: Smithsonian Institution, 1983.

Downs, James F. *The Navajo.* New York: Holt, Rinehart and Winston, 1972.

Goossen, Irvy W. *Navajo Made Easier: A Course in Conversational Navajo.* 1967. Reprint. Flagstaff, AZ: Northland Press, 1977

Faris, James C. *The Nightway: A History and a History of Documentation of a Navajo Ceremonial.* Albuquerque: University of New Mexico Press, 1990.

Haile, Father Berard, O.F.M. *Navajo Coyote Tales: The Curly Tó Aheedlínii Version.* Lincoln: University of Nebraska Press, 1984.

Iverson, Peter. *The Navajo Nation.* Albuquerque: University of New Mexico Press, 1981.

James, H.L. *Rugs and Posts: The Story of Navajo Weaving and Indian Trading.* West Chester, PA: Schiffer Publishing, 1988.

Kammer, Jerry. *The Second Long Walk: The Navajo-Hopi Land Dispute.* Albuquerque: University of New Mexico Press, 1980.

Kawano, Kenji, and Carl Gorman. *Warriors: Navajo Code Talkers.* Flagstaff, AZ: Northland Publishing, 1990.

Kelly, Klara B., and Peter M. Whiteley. *Navajoland: Family Settlement and Land Use.* Tsaile, AZ: Navajo Community College Press, 1989.

Kluckhohn, Clyde, and Dorothea Leighton. *The Navaho.* Cambridge: Harvard University Press, 1948.

Link, Martin A., ed. *Navajo: A Century of Progress 1868-1968.* Window Rock, AZ: Navajo Tribe, 1968.

Lipps, Oscar H. *A Little History of the Navajos.* Cedar Rapids, IA: Torch Press, 1909. Reprint with New Material. Albuquerque: Avanyu Publishing, 1989.

Locke, Raymond Friday. *Sweet Salt: Navajo Folktales & Mythology.* Santa Monica, CA: Roundtable Publishing Company, 1990.

————. *The Book of the Navajo.* Los Angeles: Mankind Publishing Company, 1976.

McNitt, Frank. *The Indian Traders.* Norman: University of Oklahoma Press, 1962.

Newcomb, Franc Johnson. *Navajo Omens and Taboos.* Santa Fe: Rydal Press, 1940.

Reichard, Gladys A. *Navajo Shepherd and Weaver.* Glorieta, NM: Rio Grande Press, 1936.

————. *Navaho Religion: A Study of Symbolism.* New York: Pantheon Books and Bollingen Foundation, 1950.

————. *Spiderwoman: A Story of Navajo Weavers and Chanters.* Glorieta, NM: Rio Grande Press, 1968.

Richardson, Gladwell. *Navajo Trader.* Tucson: University of Arizona Press, 1986.

Roberts, Willow. *Stokes Carson: Twentieth-Century Trading on the Navajo Reservation.* Albuquerque: University of New Mexico Press, 1987.

Roessel, Robert A., Jr. *Dinétah: Navajo History Vol. II.* Rough Rock, AZ: Navajo Curriculum Center and Rough Rock Demonstration School, 1983.

Son of Old Man Hat: A Navaho Autobiography, as recorded by Walter Dyk. Lincoln: University of Nebraska Press, 1938.

Terrell, John Upton. *The Navajos: The Past and Present of A Great People.* New York: Weybright and Talley, 1970.

Tschopik, Harry, Jr. "Taboo as a Possible Factor Involved in the Obsolescence of Navaho Pottery and Basketry." *American Anthropologist* 40, no. 2, (1938).

Underhill, Ruth. *Here Come the Navaho! A History of the Largest Indian Tribe in the United States.* Lawrence, KA: U.S. Department of the Interior, Bureau of Indian Affairs, Branch of Education, 1953.

————. *The Navajos.* Norman: University of Oklahoma Press, 1956.

Witherspoon, Gary. *Language and Art in the Navajo Universe.* Ann Arbor, MI: University of Michigan Press, 1977.

————. *Navajo Kinship and Marriage.* Chicago: University of Chicago Press, 1975.

Wyman, Leland C. *Southwest Indian Drypainting.* Santa Fe and Albuquerque: School of American Research and University of New Mexico Press, 1983.

Yazzie, Ethelou, ed. *Navajo History.* Chinle: AZ: Rough Rock Press, 1971.

Young, Robert W., and William Morgan, Sr. *The Navajo Language: A Grammar and Colloquial Dictionary.* Revised Edition. Albuquerque: University of New Mexico Press, 1987.

Zolbrod, Paul G. *Diné Bahane': The Navajo Creation Story.* Albuquerque: University of New Mexico Press, 1984.

Acknowledgments

We were the outsiders. It simply would not have been possible to have written this book without the help of a great many people—Indian traders, museum curators, gallery owners, the artists and their families—to all we are grateful and in particular:

Rex Arrowsmith, Josh Baer, Don Batchelor, Harry Batchelor, Jack and Judy Beasley, Bill Beaver, Jan Bell, Bruce Burns, Morris and Ann Butts, William Chaning, Ray Dewey, Bill Foutz, Hubert Greyeyes, Al Grieve, Robert Hake, Lynda Roscoe Hartigan, Russell Hartman, Lorena Herbert, Lucille Johnson, Mary Jones, Bob and Mariane Kapoun, Glenn and Gregg Leighton, Bruce and Ron McGee, Susan Brown McGreevy, Bill Malone, Jim and Iris Mauzy, Henri and Leslie Muth, Ed and Barbara Okun, Greg Staley, Louise Stiver, Kathy Troglea, Tsosie Tsihnahjinnie, Irving Tso, Bob and Dorothy Walker.

We also owe a debt of gratitude to Lynn Lown for his beautiful photographs of the objects and reservation scenes. This is the first time that we have had the opportunity to work with one photographer in a studio situation, and it does make a difference.

We worked closely with the staff at Northland Publishing, and without their constant encouragement, this book would not have been possible. We are indeed grateful to our editors there, Betti Albrecht and Erin Murphy, as well as Diana Clark Lubick. David Jenney supervised the design of the book and designed the backdrops for the photographs. Because of his day-by-day advice and assistance, and the talents of

designer Julie Sullivan, this project has a visual appeal worthy of the artistic accomplishments of the artists presented. And, of course, we will be forever grateful to the artists and their families. We wish them all the success in the world.

Unless otherwise indicated, the works depicted in this book are from the collection of the authors. Other credits are as follows:

Pages vii and 87—Hathale Family (attributed to Dennis Hathale), *Endless Snake,* c. 1987. Joshua Baer, Santa Fe.

Page 8—Charlie Willeto, *Male and Female Navajo Figures,* c. 1962–64. National Museum of American Art, Smithsonian Institution, gift of Herbert Waide Hemphill, Jr., and museum purchase made possible by Ralph Cross Johnson.

Page 14—Dennis Hathale, *Holy Girl, Standing Above the East and West Moon,* c. 1986. Joshua Baer, Santa Fe.

Page 29—Florence Riggs, *Dinosaur Rug,* 1992. The Carnegie Museum of Natural History, Pittsburgh.

Page 31—Robin Willeto, *Three-Headed Skinwalker,* 1991. Henri and Leslie Muth, Santa Fe.

Page 55—Charlie Willeto, *Owl,* c. 1962. William E. Channing, Santa Fe..

Page 76—Tom Yazzie, *Navajo Nativity Scene,* c. 1964. Judge and Mrs. Oliver Seth, Santa Fe.

Page 85—Hathale Family (attributed to Bruce Hathale), *Big Thunder with Four Thunderbirds,* c. 1987. Joshua Baer, Santa Fe.

Page 99—Andrew Tsihnahjinnie, *Men and Women at River,* c. 1930s. Museum of Indian Arts and Culture/ Laboratory of Anthropology, Santa Fe.

INDEX